"For years I have been fascinated by the industry legend of how Alan Watt wrote his masterful novel, *Diamond Dogs,* in 90 days. Now, at last, he shares his secrets. *The 90-Day Novel* is smart, insightful, thorough and wise. It's also one of the best books on novel writing I have ever seen. I feel confident that anyone who takes this program seriously will have a solid manuscript to show for the effort."

—DAVID LISS
(national bestselling author of
Edgar Award winner *A Conspiracy of Paper*)

"*The 90-Day Novel* is the real deal. Watt gets down to it by brilliantly articulating the fusion of the muse to the rigor of story structure. If you've been struggling with your story, or really want to get dangerous on the page, read this book. Follow it and you will have a first draft in 90 days." **—ERIC MILES WILLIAMSON**
(PEN finalist for his novel *East Bay Grease,* and author of *Say It Hot*)

"The idea of bringing a first draft of a novel to fruition seemed too daunting and overwhelming to even consider until I applied the principles in *The 90-Day Novel.* Al Watt's methodology is deep and precise, and helps unearth unconscious themes and characters in you that let the story almost tell itself."

—REBECCA DE MORNAY (actress/writer)

"*The 90-Day Novel* provides the inspiration, focus, and structure that every novelist needs to finally put down on paper what has been alive inside him, perhaps for years, struggling to get out."

—ALLISON BURNETT
(author of *Christopher,* finalist for PEN Center USA's
Literary Award in Fiction)

"*The 90-Day Novel* will guide you along the oft perilous and always enriching pathway of creative expression. Alan Watt's words are like miracle-grow for the dramatic work."

—BENJAMIN A. VAN DER VEEN
(screenwriter of Steven Soderberg's "Che:Guerilla")

PRAISE FOR LA WRITERS LAB'S
90-DAY NOVEL WORKSHOPS

"Al is a skilled and adventuresome navigator, helping me explore what lies uniquely within my subconscious. Al sends out the perfect signals to get you to the end of your novel."
—**DONNA POWERS** (screenwriter of "The Italian Job")

"The 90-Day Novel is the most fun and exhilarating feeling I have ever experienced, like falling in love. Really, I never had this feeling before, not at Harvard, not getting my book published, I don't even know how to put it into words. Al Watt is the best teacher I have ever had. He creates a space that is so safe and nurturing, I want to get it wrong because now I know I'll be able to get it right. Thank you so much, Al, for sharing what you know and your experience with me."
—**MAUREEN O'CREAN**
(author of
I Am Diva: Every Woman's Guide to Outrageous Living)

"For twelve years I struggled with writing my first novel. A friend encouraged me to sign up for the 90-Day Novel online workshop. In 90 days I have written over 150,000 words. I feel confident and alive with my writing, and happily realized I have a fantastic trilogy instead of a single novel. Who knew? I guess Al did. Now I tell everyone about the online course. Thank you Al, you've genuinely changed my life."
—**EDDIE CONNER** (radio host/author)

"Al Watt is brilliant. The 90-Day Novel online workshop gave me the structure, support and guidance to finish the first draft of a novel I'd been struggling with for a decade. Al's coaching gave me tremendous insight into the story and my characters, and the confidence that I actually could finish—which I credit as a minor miracle."
—**LAURA BRENNAN** (screenwriter)

"I went to a 'prestigious' MFA program where I eventually rewrote myself into a corner. Then I stopped writing for almost ten years. On a whim, I signed up for the 90-Day Novel workshop, and now I've left that corner for good. Through the class, I learned how to play, inquire, and access the raw material needed for my story to come alive. The act of writing has become thrilling and fun again. Thank you, Al!" —DORCAS NUNG (LMFT/90-Day Novelist)

"I met Al Watt midway through a furious deadline for my first book. It had been commissioned by Random House, but frankly, I was terrified I was going to fail—from lack of experience, knowledge of novel structure and those other private demons that prevent us from finishing (or sometimes starting) making art. Thank God for Al. I feared it would be a gung-ho course where I would be bullied into adopting certain rules—it was quite the opposite— a place where I could go and learn to trust my deepest subconscious to come up with the goods. I delivered the book on time, it's selling well, CAA has picked it up—none of this would have happened with such speed and ease without Al. Take the course!" —LUCINDA CLARE (author of the best-selling *An English Psychic in Hollywood*)

"The 90 daily letters are absolutely worth the price of admission. A friendly nudge, a gentle reminder of our commitment, a powerful blast of insight: all serve to boost our flagging morale, or comb out our confusion, or intercede with the bitter fight against our creative impulses." —MARY SHANNON (Professor of Creative Writing, Cal Sate Northridge/ 90-Day Novelist)

the 90-day novel

by
Alan Watt

A publication of The 90-Day Novel™ Press.

ISBN 978-0-9831-4120-4

DEDICATION

To all my students, past, present and future,
for sharing your vulnerability, curiosity and passion with me.
You have made me a better writer, teacher,
and someone my wife can tolerate.

TABLE OF CONTENTS

INTRODUCTION..................................xiii

PART ONE

AN OVERVIEW OF THE PROCESS...................... 3
PREPARATION....................................... 12

PART TWO

THE 90-DAY NOVEL:
THE OUTLINE EMERGES

WEEK ONE: Imagining the World of the Story
DAY 1   Imagining the World of the Story 24
DAY 2   Self-Doubt....................................... 29
DAY 3   Character Suggests Plot........................... 31
DAY 4   The Hero's Goal 33
DAY 5   The Power of Inquiry 37
DAY 6   The Structure Questions........................... 40
DAY 7   There Are No Rules.............................. 43

WEEK TWO: Story Structure
DAY 8   The Dilemma at the Heart of the Story............. 46
DAY 9   Holding Our Idea Loosely 53
DAY 10   Our Hero Takes Action/The Nature of Our Idea 55
DAY 11   What Is My Story About? 58
DAY 12   Freedom 61
DAY 13   New Ideas/Fear/Multiple Protagonists 63
DAY 14   Going Deeper................................... 68

WEEK THREE: Narrative Drive

DAY 15 Dilemma/The Plot Points/Boredom Is Resistance 72
DAY 16 The Process. 79
DAY 17 Desire. 82
DAY 18 More on Dilemma 85
DAY 19 Permission to Write the Forbidden 88
DAY 20 Story Involves a Betrayal. 90
DAY 21 Antagonists. 92

WEEK FOUR: Getting More Specific

DAY 22 Inquiry/*Diamond Dogs* Story Analysis 96
DAY 23 Our Story Is Alive 105
DAY 24 Backstory. 107
DAY 25 Movement. 109
DAY 26 Withold Judgment/Be Kind to the Artist/
          Every Open Heart Has an Antagonist. 112
DAY 27 Show, Don't Tell 115
DAY 28 The First Draft/How Long Should My Novel Be?. . . . 118

THE 90-DAY NOVEL:
WRITING THE FIRST DRAFT

WEEK FIVE: Act One—The Beginning

DAY 29 Narrative Voice. 122
DAY 30 The End Informs The Beginning/
          Belief Versus Knowing 126
DAY 31 Keep Going. 129
DAY 32 Dramatic Tension/What If My Act Two Feels Vague? 131
DAY 33 Trust The Story That Lives Within 133
DAY 34 We Cannot Make A Mistake 135
DAY 35 Self-Authority. 137

WEEK SIX: Act One—The Opposing Argument

DAY 36 I Don't Have Enough Scenes 140

DAY 37 Characters Behave Uncharacteristically 145

DAY 38 Permission to Write Poorly. 147

DAY 39 Story Structure 148

DAY 40 Humor 150

DAY 41 Our Hero Makes a Decision 152

DAY 42 Opposing Argument/Writer's Block 153

WEEK SEVEN: Act One—Our Hero Makes A Decision

DAY 43 Plot 156

DAY 44 Is My Story Going To Work?/
        What If I've Fallen Behind? 160

DAY 45 We Are Uniquely Qualified to Tell Our Story 162

DAY 46 Ughh . . . What Am I Doing? 164

DAY 47 Backstory . . . Revisited 166

DAY 48 More on the Dilemma 168

DAY 49 The Reluctant Hero/A State Of Discovery/
        The Internet: Proceed With Caution. 170

WEEK EIGHT: Act Two—Our Hero Experiences False Hope

DAY 50 Structure/Blind Spots 174

DAY 51 Asking the Right Questions 179

DAY 52 Asking "Why?" 181

DAY 53 Layering Information 183

DAY 54 Making the Scene Dynamic 185

DAY 55 Show and Tell 186

DAY 56 Be Willing to Write the Forbidden 188

WEEK NINE: The Midpoint—Our Hero Commits

DAY 57 The Midpoint: Commitment 192

DAY 58 Worthy Antagonists. 196

DAY 59 Writing Is Never a Waste of Time 198

DAY 60 Stepping Into the Unknown 200

DAY 61 Resistance 202

DAY 62 The Road to Freedom 204

DAY 63 More On the Midpoint/Temptation 206

WEEK TEN: Act Two—Our Hero Suffers

DAY 64 Story Isn't Linear 210
DAY 65 Wherein We Allow Our Hero to Suffer 213
DAY 66 From the General to the Specific 215
DAY 67 More On Suffering 217
DAY 68 More On Desire 219
DAY 69 Ten Thoughts For The Day 221
DAY 70 Courage 223

WEEK ELEVEN: Act Two—Our Hero Surrenders

DAY 71 Surrender 226
DAY 72 Making the Impossible Possible 229
DAY 73 More On Surrender 231
DAY 74 Nothing to Lose 233
DAY 75 Transformation 234
DAY 76 We Are Not Doing This Alone 236
DAY 77 The Beginning of the End 238

WEEK TWELVE: Act Three—Our Hero Takes Action

DAY 78 Reframing the Want 242
DAY 79 Accepting Reality 245
DAY 80 Surrendering Control 247
DAY 81 Why Are We Finishing Our Book? 249
DAY 82 Primal 250
DAY 83 The Hero Stripped Bare 251
DAY 84 How Do I Write My Ending? 253
DAY 85 The Battle Scene 255

THE ENDING: Act Three—Our Hero Returns Home

DAY 86 Deus Ex Machina 258
DAY 87 Story Is an Inside Job 262
DAY 88 What Our Hero Knows to Be True 264
DAY 89 Our Hero Returns Home 266
DAY 90 The End 268

PART THREE

STREAM-OF-CONSCIOUSNESS WRITING EXERCISES . . . 272
THE STRUCTURE QUESTIONS 276
ACKNOWLEDGEMENTS 279

SAMPLE OF THE 90-DAY REWRITE

AN OVERVIEW OF THE PROCESS 282

INTRODUCTION

I wrote my first novel a few years back. I had been writing for years, mostly screenplays, but with little success. I was making a decent living touring the country as a stand up comic before finally settling in Los Angeles where some managers had signed me in the hopes I would land a sitcom deal. I did get three lines on *Seinfeld*, but my dirty secret was that my comedy career was really just a means to support my writing habit.

I wanted to tell stories. The thrill of sitting alone in a room with my imagination continues to be the most satisfying experience of my life. When I started writing I was an eager student, reading every book on writing and attending every seminar along the way. However, I never believed I could write a novel. It seemed too complicated, too overwhelming, and besides, wasn't there a special novel school you had to go to? I'd never been a great student; I was too busy daydreaming, conjuring stories . . . writing. Always writing.

One day, while I was on a six-week comedy tour and without a laptop to format a screenplay, I decided to write a novel. I went to the store and bought four yellow legal pads. Armed with a story that had been swimming in my head for a while, I set a goal for myself. I would complete the first draft before the end of my forty-five day tour.

I finished the first draft on the forty-fourth day. It was around 50,000 words. I will never forget the experience of standing at the seventh-floor window of my hotel room staring down at the mid-afternoon traffic. For the first time in my life I felt like the world was no longer my enemy. I didn't know what I had written. I just remember standing at the window and wondering, "Where did that come from?" I had just accomplished something I'd previously believed was impossible. It was as if I were no longer me. When I returned to L.A., I spent the next six weeks typing my rough draft into a computer, improving it along the way. Eighty-eight days earlier I was buying paper at the pharmacy, but on that bright June day in my little studio apartment, I became a novelist.

I realized two things in retrospect: I didn't tell anyone I was writing this story, and I consciously gave myself permission to let go of the result. In fact, I had decided that I might never show the book to anyone once it was done. This freed me to write the story I had always wanted to tell without concerning myself with the opinions of others. After so many years of struggling to *make it*, and angsting over "what the market was looking for," I finally surrendered and just wrote the story, a dark tale of fathers and sons, of family secrets, of rage and redemption.

I did a quick rewrite while teaching a summer course on screenwriting at UCLA and through a lawyer friend, the manuscript found its way to an agent in New York. A week later, lo and behold, the North American rights were sold to Little, Brown for half a million dollars in a bidding war. I learned an important lesson: when we make the story more important than the result, the story has a chance to live.

I used to think that I required more confidence, but now I believe that faith is the requisite ingredient for a writer. A few years ago, *Diamond Dogs* won France's Prix Printemps (best foreign novel) and I was flown to Paris for Festival America. I sat onstage with four other writers, a Pulitzer Prize winner on my left and a National Book Award winner on my right, in front of a thousand French people, and was asked lofty questions about the author's role in the modern world. *How did I get here?!* I knew in my bones that any success I'd experienced was not the result of an intellectual process, but a willingness to surrender to the full reaches of my imagination. What the hell did I know about the novelist's role in modern society? My job was to inquire and take dictation.

One of the greatest struggles for the novice (hell, even the seasoned) writer is that we all, at times, feel like frauds. In a way, this is a good thing, because it keeps us humble. It reminds us that we are simply channels for our story and that when we listen and inquire, real truths emerge.

The 90-Day Novel is not a book about how to sell a novel, nor is it a course designed to fine-tune your pitch, perfect your book proposal, get an agent, or meet a publisher. All of those topics are valuable, I'm sure, but as my agent says, "Until you have written your novel, you have nothing to sell." *The 90-Day Novel* is an opportunity to go deep, to let it rip, to write the story you have always wanted to tell. When we allow the thrill of creation to be its own reward, we are often surprised by the result.

AL WATT
Los Angeles
March, 2010

PART ONE

the 90-day novel

AN OVERVIEW OF THE PROCESS

The 90-Day Novel Workshop was born out of necessity. I had been teaching my ongoing workshops for years and was growing frustrated that some of the writers were taking years to complete the first drafts of their novels. They were having lots of fun in class, but it was apparent that for some, the class was the extent of their writing for the week. Although I encouraged them to write their first drafts quickly, there was no system in place to support this goal. The deadlines I gave them didn't seem to make a difference. I knew that when I started writing my first drafts quickly, I stopped censoring myself and the work sprang to life. It took me around three months to write a first draft. It's long enough to get plenty of words down but not so long that we get buried by perfectionism. Stephen King writes his first drafts in three months. John Steinbeck banged out his first draft of *The Grapes of Wrath* in roughly ninety days. Over and over, we hear writers talk about the importance of getting the first draft down quickly. When we write quickly, we tend to bypass our critical voices and tap directly into the heart of our story.

It came to me: The 90-Day Novel.

I put out the word and the workshop filled up quickly. I rented a space at the Black Dahlia Theater on Pico Boulevard, wondering to myself if this was even going to work. Some of these people had never written before, while others had struggled for years on the same story. I feared I might be setting them up for disappointment. I decided to throw myself into it, and leave the results to the gods.

There was a weird giddiness in the group. They weren't fretting over how difficult it would be; instead they asked, "Isn't this impossible?" And I thought to myself . . . um, yeah. It struck me that when we are confronted with the impossible, we let go of our expectations and that's when miracles tend to happen. When the focus shifts from "Will it be good?" to "Will it get done?" our subconscious is free to do its work, and that work often bears rich fruit.

The excitement of the group was palpable. We had made a contract with our subconscious to complete a task that held a tremendous amount of meaning for us. A camaraderie quickly formed on the private group page, and although writing is a solitary act, the willingness of each writer to share his daily victories as well as his private demons created a spirit of support and encouragement that pulled everyone along in its wake.

Of the fourteen writers who signed up, only two did not complete their first drafts. (One has returned to work with me privately after a two-year hiccup, and the other dropped out early for personal reasons.) Which is to say that virtually every student that signed up completed their novel in 90 days!

SO, WHY DID I HAVE TROUBLE BEFORE?

It doesn't help that we live in a left-brain society. We have been trained to second-guess ourselves, to be more interested in the result than the process. We are not encouraged to be curious, so it's difficult to really get quiet and inquire. The decision to be creative is often met with concern, suspicion, and even outright scorn. Can you imagine telling your folks, "Well, I waffled between med school and law school, but I've decided to write tone poems"?

The prevailing attitude is that if you're not great at something right out of the gate, then you shouldn't bother. This type of thinking prevents countless creative people from ever getting started. Quite simply, the desire to write is connected to the desire to evolve. We are here to express ourselves. Creativity is not an occupation; it is our birthright. It is a way for us to make meaning of our lives, to reframe our relationship to the world, to communicate the deepest aspects of ourselves.

And quite frankly, most books about writing novels miss the point. They tend to be technical and dispassionate, and are often written by blocked creatives who shed their imaginations in graduate school. The *advice* is not even benign— it's actually counterproductive, because so many of these books are result-oriented and actually pull you out of your imagination! I did find Walter Mosely's book *This Year You Write Your Novel*, informative and inspiring, and I devoured Stephen King's quasi-memoir *On Writing*. Stories are alive. They are nonlinear. The moment we leave our right brains, we're dead in the water.

This book speaks unabashedly to your heart, not for sentimental reasons, but because this is where our stories reside. Why we write is as important as what we write. Grammar, punctuation and syntax are fairly irrelevant in the first draft. Get the story down . . . fast. Get out of your head, so you can surprise yourself on the page.

START WHERE YOU ARE

Our job as artists is to build a body of work. When we drop our preconceptions about what good writing is and we give ourselves permission to write poorly, everything changes. Permission to write poorly does not produce poor writing, but its opposite. We become a channel for the story that wants to be told through us. Rather than impressing our reader with our important writing, we can impress with our willingness to be truthful on the page.

IMAGINING THE WORLD OF THE STORY

The first step in *The 90-Day Novel* process is simply imagining the world of our story. When we attempt to plot out our story, we may likely find ourselves writing our idea of the story. It's not that our idea is wrong, it's just that it is probably not the whole story. The story resides in our subconscious, and when we allow our subconscious a period of time to play, our characters tend to spring to life and surprise us with where they want to go. Imagining the world means imagining our characters in relationship to each other and scribbling down the images, ideas and fragments of dialogue that emerge. I have created a lengthy series of stream-of-consciousness writing exercises (found on page 272) that have proved helpful in allowing the world of the story to emerge. When we write what truly interests us, conflict arises.

CONFLICT

Conflict is central to drama. As we imagine the world of our story, we are naturally drawn to charged moments both large and small. We are not going to be drawn to what our hero had for breakfast . . . unless he's on death row and it is his final meal.

All we need to do at this stage in the process is to very quickly scribble down whatever comes to us. It is thrilling to sit in front of the page and allow images to accumulate without having to immediately force them into our *idea* of our story. We want to allow ourselves a period of time to just explore these budding scenarios without making premature demands on a plot. As we remain curious and continue to write, more questions emerge and a world forms.

Let's be clear: at this stage, we are not writing our novel, nor are we even outlining our story. We are simply allowing our right brain to play, to make connections we will only comprehend in retrospect. Without this initial step, outlining the story can become an exercise in limiting our options. We never want our idea of our story to get in the way of letting our characters live. There may even be times when it seems like we are going in the wrong direction. Rather than panicking, we can inquire into the nature of our experience and be curious about where this experience exists in the world of our story. As we allow our characters to live, we are able to explore the vastness of their choices.

HOLDING IT LOOSELY

Again, we are not structuring our story yet. We are just allowing our mind to wander around in the world of our story and writing down whatever emerges.

For example, let's say I begin with the bare bones of an idea: I want to write a love story set in New York. I might wonder where these two people live, what their backgrounds are, and how they are going to meet. Hmmm. Okay. Jack lives on the Upper East Side and Jill lives in . . . the Bronx. Hmmm . . . I like that. That feels interesting. What else? Well, how do they meet? What if she is a bank robber and he is a lawyer? Maybe. What else? Well, he could be a banker. Possibly, but it feels sort of obvious and like something Elmore Leonard has done a million times. What if they meet in an elevator? And the power goes out? Hmmm. I kind of like that. What if they are on their way to divorce court (wow, where did that come from?) and they are both getting divorces and they meet at their divorce trial? Oh, wow. What if it is two couples and they start dating the other one's former spouse immediately following their respective divorces? Ooh, that's interesting—it brings up the question—did the marriage fail because of her or him? Whose fault is it? Or were they just poorly matched? Hmm . . . I like that.

Okay. So . . . I just scribbled that down in about four or five minutes—completely random, playing on the page. I just want to give you a sense of the experience of allowing your imagination to wander. If I were to continue writing, the premise might shift in all sorts of directions. I am simply trusting my curiosity. The moment we force it, or fear that we are getting it wrong, we're out of our story. One of the real challenges of this process is accepting the satisfaction that accompanies it. We aren't writing at this stage, we are scribbling, allowing ourselves to dream on the page.

FROM THE GENERAL TO THE SPECIFIC

When we hold our ideas loosely, we can move very quickly, discarding one idea for another. Can you imagine if I decided early on that Jill was a bank robber and then started writing my novel? I would have eliminated all of the possibilities that followed. I would have immediately narrowed my options. And frankly, that is not the story I wanted to tell. It may have been my original idea—bank robber and banker, but, in fact, what I discovered was really interesting to me was the nature of an antagonistic romantic relationship. For my purposes, it may be more effective if I have two newly divorced couples and they swap partners. The nature of the relationship has not changed but the premise feels stronger as a means of exploring this question (a question I was not even conscious of a minute earlier).

There is enormous value to imagining the world of our story prior to writing it or even outlining it. We don't have to waste weeks and months writing hundreds of pages about a banker and his nefarious sweetheart only to realize that our interest is waning. When we move from the general to the specific, we are far less inclined to write six-hundred pages only to discover that our story lacks a narrative drive.

Our subconscious is really good at making order out of chaos, and so our job is to give it conflict in the form of a story. It will go right to work, even in our sleep. As a sense of the world begins to reveal itself through imagining our characters in relationship to each other, we start asking the simple question, "I wonder what might happen next?" Scenarios begin to reveal themselves.

We are starting to get a sense of the world, but we have not limited ourselves by making any demands on what must happen. There may be all sorts of disparate images and situations that seem to contradict each other. That's okay. We are not writing our story yet. Oftentimes these apparent contradictions are leading us to deeper truths and if we were to start outlining right off the bat, we would never have allowed ourselves this depth of character. We are complex creatures; our behavior is often utterly illogical, yet at the same time it makes perfect sense. Once we begin to develop a sense of the world of our story, we can begin to inquire into the structure questions.

THE STRUCTURE QUESTIONS

The structure questions (found on page 276) are designed to invite images up from our subconscious at key points in our hero's journey. When we ask universal questions, over time the framework of a story emerges. As we continue to inquire, a beginning, middle and ending reveal themselves to us. Nothing is forced through this process. Some of the images that emerge may seem wildly disconnected from each other. You might think, "How on earth is my hero going to go from driving a truck in Memphis to singing on the Ed Sullivan Show?" But as we continue to inquire into the structure questions, and we hold our story loosely, it becomes more specific.

The structure questions open us up to our subconscious, that deep knowing that stretches our imagination beyond the personal to the universal, places that might feel a little too exotic and frightening and just plain not nice to our well-brought-up selves. I sometimes witness writers limiting their stories by judging their characters, as if human beings ever navigated the world through logic. I've seen writers kill the conflict in their stories with statements like, 'Well, I can't have him cheat on his wife. If he got caught the consequences would be dire.' Great! Let them be dire! Get excited about the conflict in your story, the sticky situations in which your characters lose themselves.

Don't ever worry about putting your characters into situations that you can't *figure* a way out of. It is not your job to figure it out. Trust that your subconscious will find a way to resolve it. Remember, this process is not linear. Allow yourself to be surprised by the wildness of your characters' choices. Our job is to stay connected to what it is that our hero wants and to simply support the resulting actions. There is nothing logical about infidelity, high-speed chases, falling in love, climbing Mount Everest, or committing high treason, but these things happen every day.

THE OUTLINE

As we explore the structure questions while continuing to imagine the world of our story, a series of images begin to appear. There is not yet a clear through-line, but there is a connection to the source, a sense that our characters are not merely functions of a plot, but are really, truly alive. As we continue to imagine, we may wonder, "How on earth does my character get from Portugal to Canada?" or, "I had no idea he spoke Farsi!" or, "Wow, why would she ask for a divorce when she just learned that she was pregnant?" We trust the images that are revealed. We relax and allow our subconscious to do the work. Storytelling is a right-brain activity. The moment we attempt to come up with logical solutions to human behavior, we are out of our story.

EVERYONE'S PROCESS IS DIFFERENT

There are no rules. The creative process is as mysterious and as personal as each of us. It is about trusting our instincts in the face of self-doubt. Some people feel comfortable with a thorough outline before writing their first draft. Some writers want to outline very little and begin with the loosest sense of where the story wants to take them. Ultimately, the choice is our own.

Within this process, you will find your own rhythm. I'm simply imparting the principles to you. How you apply them will be discovered and refined over a lifetime.

WRITING THE FIRST DRAFT

After we have spent the first four weeks imagining the world and allowing an outline to emerge, a story begins to reveal itself. Armed with a sense of a beginning, middle and end, we can begin writing our first draft. We are going to write the first draft quickly. When we pause to edit, we tend to get stuck.

We are going to set small goals for ourselves based on the plot points from our outlines. We will write to these goals each week, and by doing so we will reach the end of our first draft by Day 90.

Okay. Breathe.

PREPARATION

We are almost ready to begin writing our 90-Day Novel. Let's just do a few quick writing exercises to explore the world of our story. Our goals with these exercises are as follows:

- To recognize why we are uniquely qualified to write our story.

- To reframe our fears and use them as a way into our work.

- To develop a primal relationship to our story. Every story has a narrative drive. The narrative drive is not the plot, but the underlying meaning that drives the plot.

- To develop a relationship to the antagonists in our story. Without a clear sense of the antagonistic forces, we'll be in bondage to our fixed ideas of the story.

Let's get started.

THE FEAR EXERCISE

 Write for five minutes, as fast as you can, beginning with the sentence:

"I'm afraid to write this story because . . ."

Nothing is too trivial. And be willing to write the forbidden. Make a list of all of your fears.

Go.

OK. Great. Now write that one last fear you didn't feel like putting down on paper.

Fantastic!

Why do we do this exercise? The first reason is fairly obvious; by acknowledging our fears, we are no longer ruled by them.

The second reason is that the fears we experience are **identical to the fears our protagonist experiences.** We are always telling our story on some level. If we interpret our fears literally, we may not get far with this exercise. However, if we inquire into the nature of our fears, we will begin to recognize all sorts of connections between ourselves and our protagonist. Our fears make us uniquely qualified to write our story.

Many common fears include:

- I will fail.
- I will succeed.
- My family will hate me.
- I will discover I'm not really a writer.
- I will discover that I am a writer and then I'll have to keep doing this.
- I will die.
- I am wasting my time.
- I am not good enough.
- It will be superficial.
- I won't be able to figure it out.
- I won't do it right.
- I will find out I am a bad person.
- Nobody will care.
- I will be alone.

This is a short list, but my guess is that you can probably

relate to a few of these. Can you make a connection between your fears and the fears of your protagonist? Is he afraid to fail? Is he afraid that he won't be good enough? Is he afraid that if he takes up the challenge, he will be alone?

We may have been using our fears as a reason not to write, perhaps even waiting for them to subside before proceeding. Every writer has fear. If we give ourselves permission to write from this raw, vulnerable place, our work becomes instantly relatable. It becomes universal. I encourage you to get excited by your fears. Make friends with them. They offer clues, and direct access into your story.

EVERY HERO HAS A CODE

If you've ever seen a Western or read a Raymond Chandler novel, you know that cowboys and detectives live by a code. Their code may not make sense to others, but it sure as heck does to them. They live by their code, and die by it too. Their code is a metaphor for their spirit, for something larger than themselves. They are willing to die for something. These characters are archetypes, primal forces we can all relate to.

We all have a code.

What do we believe in with such conviction that nothing could sway us from fighting for it to the death? Is it freedom, truth, justice, loyalty, friendship, love, authenticity, self-authority, the limited rights of the left-handed . . . okay, you get my point. It's unlimited.

Write for five minutes:
"One thing I feel strongly about is . . ."

Write as fast as you can. Do not lift your pen off the page. And it's just ONE thing you feel strongly about. Do not write a list! And *feel* is the operative word. Tell us why you feel strongly about this.

Go.

Okay. Excellent work! By writing what we feel strongly about, we may notice a connection between the story we want to write and this thing we care so deeply about. Remember, the desire to write is the desire to evolve, to resolve something we seek to understand.

What we feel strongly about is necessarily subjective, meaning that it has an opposing argument. We don't feel strongly about facts. I don't feel strongly that I'm sitting in a chair or that I had peanut butter on toast for breakfast. When we inquire into what we feel strongly about, we begin to get a sense of the opposing arguments. I feel strongly about justice, but exactly what is justice? Who determines it? Is it based on a single standard or is it culturally determined? In some societies a woman is killed for leaving her abusive husband. Is that just? According to whom?

By inquiring into what we feel strongly about, we are led directly to the seed of a powerful story. At this point, we may have just the thinnest idea of a story, but this exercise will help us begin to recognize the themes we are exploring. Writers often revisit the same themes throughout their careers, examining them from various points of view. Hemingway was drawn repeatedly to questions of honor and manhood. Fitzgerald was drawn to issues of class and the elusiveness of the American dream. It's important for us to become conscious of what we feel strongly about and begin to explore its opposite, because this will lead us directly into the conflict.

By inquiring into what we feel strongly about, we begin to get a sense of our antagonists. It is character that suggests plot. We don't have to figure out our story. As we inquire into the nature of our characters, images, ideas and situations develop. Without powerful opposing arguments, our antagonists will be two-dimensional and the conflict will flatline.

Stories are about transformation. Transformation simply means a shift in perception. In order for our protagonist to arrive at a shift in perception, our story requires powerful antagonists to stand in the way of him achieving his goal. Story is alchemy. It is through the struggle between our protagonist and his antagonists that he is transformed.

Writers sometimes tell me that they just want to write a cute little story. That's fine. The stakes are still life and death for your characters. If your protagonist does not fulfill his goal, his life will be unimaginable. This is not about tone or genre. If the stakes are not life and death, no one will care about your characters. Not even you.

What we feel strongly about is that thing we want to stand on our rooftop and shout to the world, that thing we would die for, that thing we are uniquely qualified to express. What we feel strongly about is not the plot, but rather the underlying meaning that drives the plot.

What is that thing? Be curious. Because that is what your story is about.

THE DILEMMA AT THE HEART OF THE STORY

A dilemma is a problem that can't be solved without creating another problem. At the heart of every story is a dilemma. If we're not sure what our story is about, let's consider this for a moment: Problems are solved while dilemmas are resolved through a shift in perception.

Einstein said, *"You can't solve a problem at the same level of consciousness that created the problem."* Every story begins with an *apparent* problem. Susie Salmon is raped and murdered at the beginning of Alice Sebold's *The Lovely Bones.* A boy and his father are struggling to survive in Cormac McCarthy's *The Road.* But as we scratch the surface, we see that in fact, underlying these problems are dilemmas and this is what the story is really about. *The Lovely Bones* is not about a rape and murder. It's about the desire for connection and the pain of letting go. Susie yearns for a connection with her family that she can never have, and yet she cannot say goodbye. We can all relate to being in that place between desire and surrender. In *The Road*, a boy and his father struggle to survive in a post-apocalyptic world. The story is about how to hold onto our humanity in the face of fear. The characters are functions of this dramatic question. The boy is an innocent, questioning his father's ideas and behavior. He represents hope. The father keeps him safe, but it is only in the end when the father is gone that the boy is free to trust the people who take him in.

Life is full of dilemmas. *Revolutionary Road* and *The Catcher in the Rye* illustrate that the desire to belong is at war with the desire to be an individual. In Suzanne Collin's *The Hunger Games* and Charles Baxter's *The Feast of Love* the desire for love is at war with the desire to maintain autonomy and/or survive.

Be curious about the dilemma at the heart of your story, and don't panic if you can't figure this out. It's more important to be curious and develop a relationship to it than it is to answer it. We're not looking for answers—we're looking for an alive relationship to the world of our story. If we're unsure, we can just explore an image that we have for our story. It will likely be charged. We can be curious about the circumstances and ask ourselves what the conflict is. The conflict will lead us to the heart of the dilemma.

Write for five minutes, beginning with: "The dilemma at the heart of my story is . . ."

When we recognize that our hero does not have a problem but rather, a dilemma, our story begins to wake up. If our hero has an impossible problem, how the hell are we going to solve it?

We're not. And neither is he. He's going to surrender. He's going to reframe his relationship to what he wants and in doing so, he is going to begin to work with the reality of his situation.

A dilemma is at the heart of every story, from Dr. Seuss to Tolstoy. It creates the narrative drive. New writers often want to control the process by believing that their protagonist has a problem that is difficult to solve but not impossible. Let's be clear: our protagonist doesn't have a problem. He only thinks he does. He has a dilemma. A problem, in and of itself, will not get our hero to the end of the story. The meaning he makes out of his *apparent* problem is the engine that drives the story. I have worked with countless writers and I can tell you that the primary reason they get stuck in the middle of their story is because they either fail to recognize or accept this. When you inquire into the dilemma, you are literally tapping into a wellspring of images, ideas and situations that, through the structure questions, will lead your hero on a journey to transformation. When we begin to understand that the resolution to our story is arrived at by simply inquiring into the nature of the dilemma, our perspective widens and unimagined possibilities emerge.

LET'S GET STARTED

A FEW FINAL HINTS:

1. Don't talk about your story to others. Talking about it dissipates the urgency to write it. Contain the energy.

2. OK, you've talked about it. To everyone. They will ask you how it's going. Say nothing. Carry your story with you like a delicious secret. Oftentimes artists who have had their first creative breakthrough want to proclaim it to the world. This is called self-sabotage. Keep quiet and keep writing. Which sounds better? "Yeah, I just finished writing a novel," or "I'm writing a novel."

3. Commit yourself to a time to write each day. We are creatures of habit.

4. I suggest writing two hours a day. Every day. Two hours will get you to the end.

5. Find a quiet place to work. Do this ahead of time.

6. Clear the decks. For the next 90 days: don't get married, divorced, add a second floor to your house, or move across the country. Let's give ourselves every opportunity to succeed.

7. Lastly, every writer who begins this workshop is terrified. You are not alone. Your fear is an indication that this story holds a tremendous amount of meaning for you. Through this process, you are going to work with your fear, and I will guide you every step of the way.

What follows is a day-by-day process designed to lead you through the hero's journey and get you to the end of your first draft. Writers tell me that the 90-Day Letters often uncannily reflect their daily experience. As well as being a guide through the process, they are also a response to the hundreds of writers who have logged on daily to the private group page and shared their experiences in the *90-Day Novel* workshops over the past three years.

Some of the material is intentionally repetitive. This is an intuitive process and some of the fundamental principles bear repeating.

Let's begin.

His dilemma - getting "home" means giving up the home he knew: cannot return to his old configuration: letting go illusion he can save them by returning, and rather he will save himself when he allows this new unit to be home

they will save him

the 90-day novel

WEEK 1

IMAGINING THE WORLD
OF THE STORY

During this week we will inquire into the nature of our premise and allow images and ideas to emerge. This is primarily a right-brain process. If we allow our subconscious some time to play without imposing any structural limitations, our characters tend to surprise us, affording us more dynamic possibilities when we begin to outline. On Day 4 we begin to inquire into the structure questions.

DAY 1

"Imagination is more important than knowledge. Knowledge is limited. Imagination encircles the world."   —**ALBERT EINSTEIN**

IMAGINING THE WORLD OF THE STORY

Hi Writers,

This week is all about stream-of-consciousness writing, or *playing on the page.* We will not officially begin writing the first drafts of our novels until Day 29. This week our goal is to develop a more specific relationship to the world of our story. The first four weeks of stream-of-consciousness writing allow a basic outline to emerge. Remember, this is not a process of *figuring out* our story. In fact, it is important at this stage to allow our subconscious free rein without imposing any limitations. We are simply imagining our characters in relationship to each other and scribbling down the images and ideas that emerge. At this point we may likely only have a general sense of our story, and that is exactly where we need to be.

Writing isn't something that happens outside of ourselves. Our story lives within. When we're feeling confused, scared, excited or hopeful, we can ask ourselves, "Where does this experience exist in the world of my story?" The nature of the experience may reveal an image or a situation that informs our story. It might be helpful to have a visual sense of what I mean by stream-of-consciousness writing. My notebooks are nearly illegible. I don't cross anything out. I don't concern myself with punctuation. I am literally downloading images and ideas as quickly as possible, in no narrative fashion. I am searching for the aliveness in my story. There are no rules here. I am simply filling the well with images. At some point, perhaps after a couple of hours, I become tired and feel like I have run out of ideas. The next morning, something miraculous tends to happen. When I wake up, new images and ideas have already developed upon what I scribbled down the day before. I used to worry that I would run out of ideas; after years of experiencing this phenomenon, I trust the process. When we sleep, our subconscious remains active, making connections and puzzling over our story's dilemma. We are not in charge of this process. All we need to do is relax, sit at the table, and inquire. Our inner genius does the rest.

It's important to understand that we cannot *figure out* our plot and drop our characters into it. It doesn't work like that. Character and plot are inextricably linked. They inform each other. Our characters are defined through the actions they take, and their actions are informed by their attempts to get what they want. By sitting quietly and imagining our characters in relation to each other, conflict will naturally emerge. We begin to *see* situations and very quickly write down what we see. Some of the situations may seem contradictory but that is OK because we are not yet writing our story. If we can hold it all loosely at this point and just give ourselves permission to explore the world, we will begin to fill the well with all sorts of images that we can draw from when we start to write our first draft. The world of our story is not *the story*—it can't be—we don't know what the story is yet. We may have an idea of what it is, but if we can hold that idea loosely it will allow for some of these seemingly disparate images and ideas to cohere.

The purpose of story is to reveal a transformation. When we allow seemingly disparate ideas to coexist, a synthesis tends to occur. These ideas begin to resolve themselves and we are led to a deeper truth. This is the purpose of the next four weeks. Through inquiry we are gradually going to develop a more specific relationship to the story that wants to be told through us.

On page 272 you will find a series of stream-of-consciousness writing exercises. Sometimes, after a while we may get bored, or feel like we're circling the same ideas. These writing prompts can often reconnect us to the primal nature of our story and take us in new directions. I strongly suggest that you use them every day until you are ready to begin writing your first draft.

Lastly, outlining is often taught as a left-brain endeavor, as if it is our job to figure out our story. Not only is it not our job, I frankly don't believe it is possible. Einstein says, "We cannot solve a problem at the same level of consciousness that created the problem." It's the same with story—we can't solve the problem of our story, but what we can do is inquire into our characters at various stages in our hero's journey (which we will begin doing on Day 4) and allow our subconscious to build a bridge to that place where our hero experiences a shift in perception. If we were to try and figure all of this out now, we would simply throw our hands up in frustration. Our job at this stage is to simply imagine our characters in relation to each other, write down the images and ideas that emerge, and when we get bored, write for five minutes or so on the stream-of-consciousness writing exercises.

WRITING EXERCISES FOR THE DAY:

Write for five minutes, beginning with . . .

1. "My story is about . . ."

2. "What I want to express through this story is . . ."

Until tomorrow,
Al

WEEK 1: THOUGHTS AND REMINDERS

- There are no rules. We cannot make a mistake.

- The story lives fully and completely within us.

- We are uniquely qualified to tell our story.

- This is a process of learning to trust our inner voice. It's not about being a good student.

- Our idea of the story is not the whole story. It's not that our ideas are wrong, but rather that through inquiry, a more fully realized story emerges.

- The desire to write is connected to the desire to evolve. Our fears are a way into our story.

- What our hero wants is connected to an idea of what it will give him. Example: "When I win the marathon I will gain respect."

- Story is about transformation.

- As writers, our job is to track the beats in a compelling and believable way that leads to a transformation.

- There is a dilemma for our hero at the heart of our story. This is where the tension lies.

- Character suggests plot.

- The thrill of creation must be its own reward.

- This process is like a developing Polaroid photo. Over time, through inquiry, our story comes into focus.

HOMEWORK FOR THE WEEK

1. Do the daily writing exercises.

2. Imagine the world of your story. You are developing a deeper relationship to your story through writing down images, ideas, situations, and fragments of dialogue.

3. When you get bored imagining the world of your story, explore the stream-of-consciousness writing exercises at the back of the book. They are in no particular order. Choose any one of them and keep writing. Repeat them as often as you like. They are not questions to be answered, they are exercises designed to trigger your imagination and help you develop a primal relationship to your characters. The goal is simply to keep your pen moving for two hours each day, filling the well with material that you can draw from when you begin writing your first draft on Day 29.

4. On Day 4 you will begin exploring the structure questions.

DAY 2

"And by the way, everything in life is writable about if you have the outgoing guts to do it, and the imagination to improvise. The worst enemy to creativity is self-doubt."   —SYLVIA PLATH

SELF-DOUBT

Hi Writers,

After committing to a creative project we often become inexplicably riddled with self-doubt. If we find ourselves thinking that our stories are not interesting enough, not comparable to the work of someone we admire, or even just plain silly, we are probably experiencing a little garden-variety resistance.

We are not writing our story yet. We don't even know what it will look or sound like, so how could we possibly judge it? What makes a story special is not so much what happens but rather the specificity through which the world is conveyed. Our willingness to write truthfully brings the story to life.

At this point, our only job is to inquire into the world of our story. Sometimes our story lies a few feet beneath a layer of hard earth. We may need to hack our way through some old ideas before we hit the truth. It might take a moment before we start to feel a flow; stay loose and continue to inquire, remembering that you are uniquely qualified to tell your story.

This is a major shift for some of us. We are dropping our

defenses and this can be scary. We must keep on writing those images, ideas, and fragments of dialogue as fast as we can, and if we find ourselves running out of steam, we can investigate our worthy antagonists. Our worthy antagonists are any characters that stand in the way of our hero getting what he wants. They are not necessarily villains. Exploring our hero in conflict with an antagonist will reveal more images and ideas. We are not plotting our story, we are simply imagining the world and allowing it to appear.

Think about the way a child tells a story. When you ask him a question, he delivers an answer without hesitation. It is with this spirit of boldness that we inquire into our world. There are no wrong answers. Children have complete confidence in their narrative. They are fearless, lost in the bliss of their imaginations. Their motivation is to delight themselves. As we amuse ourselves, we will naturally move in the direction of our story.

Lastly, the antidote to self-doubt is not steeling oneself against it, but simply writing through it. Make friends with it. Inquire into its nature. If I am scared, I can ask myself where this particular fear lives in the world of my story. The fear is there for a reason. When we begin to work with our doubts and fears, we grow as storytellers, recognizing that our circumstances are not overcome through force of will but by acceptance.

WRITING EXERCISES FOR THE DAY:

1. Write for five minutes as your hero, beginning with the phrase . . . "You would never know this by looking at me, but. . ."

2. Write for five minutes as your hero, beginning with . . . "Every time I think I'm going to get what I want, it seems that . . ."

3. Write for five minutes as your hero, beginning with . . . "I need to be forgiven for . . ."

Until tomorrow,
Al

DAY 3

"We take care of the quantity, and we let God take care of the quality."   —JULIA CAMERON

CHARACTER SUGGESTS PLOT

Hi Writers,

As we inquire into our characters, situations and fragments of dialogue are revealed that lead us to further inquiry. We ask, "What happens next?" We don't have to know how or where these images fit into our story. At this point our concern is staying connected to the aliveness of our story. We can feel the tensions, the painful unmet desires. Perhaps we are starting to glimpse the complex dances at play and on a subconscious level are beginning to sense the core dilemma that lies at the heart of our story. It is not important to be able to articulate it, but rather to be aware of the feeling that there's a problem that can never be solved. We don't ever try to solve the problem of our story because it isn't possible. At the heart of the apparent problem is a dilemma. Problems can be solved, while dilemmas can only be resolved through a shift in perception.

What defines our characters are the choices they make. Our characters are functions of the story. This is why character sketches are sort of a waste of time, the implication being that characters exist in a vacuum, that their behavior is static and predictable and based on a set of predetermined traits. But as Malcolm Gladwell states in his book *Blink*, human beings behave situationally, not characteristically. Imagining the world of the story allows for our characters to surprise us, to respond in ways that are in keeping with our first impulses.

Writing is an act of faith, but it's not an act of blind faith. We have faith in the story within. As we work with our story over time, we begin to discover that the possibilities are infinite. Our story can contain anything we imagine once it is distilled to the nature of what we're trying to say. Story structure is not a formula. Formulas are predictable. There is nothing predictable about a well-told story. The hallmark of skilled writing is the ability to track the beats in a compelling and believable way that leads to a transformation. This ability is simply the result of rigorous inquiry and a willingness to put our curiosity before the result.

Transformation is nothing more than a shift in perception. A shift in perception does not necessarily mean a happy ending. Freedom from the bondage of an idea does not necessarily mean that the boy gets the girl. Sometimes we only see the light as darkness descends.

WRITING EXERCISES FOR TODAY:

1. Write for five minutes as your hero, beginning with . . . "One thing you still need to know about me is . . ." Write as if your hero were telling you a secret about herself. Surprise yourself. Let it rip. Be willing to write the forbidden.

2. Now do this for an antagonist in your story. Do it for any character you wish. Be willing to let go of your idea of who your characters are, and let them tell you. What do they want you to know?

Until tomorrow,
Al

DAY 4

"If you greatly desire something, have the guts to stake everything on obtaining it."
—BRENDAN FRANCIS BEHAN

THE HERO'S GOAL

Hi Writers,

We hear a lot of talk about the hero needing to be likeable. Likeability is subjective. Attempting to make a character likeable can be a sure way to kill the aliveness of our story. We care about the hero because he wants something . . . anything. Our hero's goal is primal. A strong goal pulls us into the story.

Does our hero want love, revenge, approval, respect, security, validation, hope, meaning, comfort, answers, fame, wealth, to conquer . . . all of the above? The desire/motivation/goal is the engine that drives our story. When it is primal, the stakes are life and death and we cannot help but be invested in the outcome.

Imagine every possible way your hero could get what he wants. And remember that your story has a worthy antagonist. Every time your hero takes a step forward, the antagonist is right there, standing in his way. It's a dance. It's not linear. Our hero's want never changes, never falters. However, the way he approaches getting what he wants is constantly changing as a result of his relationship to his antagonists.

Let's say our hero wants love. As we explore this problem

we begin to recognize that the search for love is a setup. For example: the more I try to get a person to love me, the more I may repel that person, or, they may fall for me and I no longer respect him or her for being attracted to my neediness. A dilemma begins to reveal itself and we begin to glimpse the infinite possibilities within this complicated dance.

All of our characters function as potential tools in exploring the nature of the dilemma at the heart of our story. So perhaps what our hero learns in his search for love is that he doesn't need to find love outside of himself, but rather within. Sounds obvious perhaps, clichéd even, but it can be the stuff of great fiction.

Our hero doesn't need to find love. It is not something he lost. It is readily available. By surrendering his want (which is different than giving up) he starts to love himself. And the irony is that it then becomes possible for him to have love with someone, if that person belongs in his life.

THE STRUCTURE QUESTIONS

The structure questions (found on page 276) are connected to our hero's journey. Let's ask these questions and write for a few minutes on each one. We are not *answering* them, but rather allowing our imaginations to inquire. We want to approach these questions with a spirit of curiosity. Let's allow ourselves to have fun, to take risks, to make wild choices, and always, to hold it all loosely. We are after a sense of aliveness and surprise.

We are not expected to have a fully worked-out story by next week—far from it! We are just going to play on the page, explore and be curious about the journey. Characters will appear to us from out of nowhere. We will allow them to exist. We will remain curious and write it all down. Where they come from is none of our business. If this seems too easy, we don't question it. If it seems overwhelming, we stop thinking and give ourselves permission to write poorly. We are engaged in a process of trusting our subconscious to reveal the story to us. Our job is to remain curious.

We tend to judge our work prematurely, without giving it time to gestate. I believe that this process is the most efficient approach to getting a fully realized story onto the page. It's also the most thrilling because we are letting go of much unnecessary angst. It doesn't mean that feelings don't come up, but we can put our neuroses on the backburner. We focus on getting the story onto the page without making judgments about its quality. When we work in this way, our subconscious is free to do its work, and that work often bears rich fruit.

I repeat: Don't concern yourselves with an outline this week.

Even as we start to write our novels, we can trust that what we need to know will reveal itself to us in time. All we have to do is sit for two hours a day and trust the process.

Be curious about the moment your hero makes a decision to go after getting what he wants. In this moment he leaves the security of the familiar for the unknown. In Judith Guest's novel *Ordinary People*, Calvin Jarrett speaks up to his wife for the first time, disagreeing with her about his choice to tell a friend that their son is seeing a psychologist. Calvin wants to have a happy family; in that moment, he steps out of what had been familiar and toward a new way of being. Guided consciously or unconsciously by his want, he begins the journey toward considering himself.

The decision that your hero can't go back on may not look anything like you think it should. You may wonder how disagreeing with one's wife could be an attempt to create a happy family. There is nothing logical about human behavior. Logic is shallow. The truth of our nature is primal.

Note: Do not try to *solve* any of the structure questions. It's more important to just inquire and to trust that your story lives fully and completely within you, that all of the juicy, exciting madness you wish to express absolutely belongs in your story.

WRITING EXERCISES FOR TODAY:

As your hero, write for five minutes . . .

1. "The answer to my problem I've been avoiding is . . ."

2. "If I could do one thing differently from my past, it would be . . ."

3. Lastly, today begin inquiring into the structure questions. Write quickly. Surprise yourself.

Until tomorrow,
Al

DAY 5

"The truth will set you free. But first it will kick your ass."   **—UNKNOWN**

THE POWER OF INQUIRY

Hi Writers,

This process is about moving from the general to the specific. As we imagine our characters in relationship to each other, a more specific relationship to our story develops. This process should feel loose and fun. We are filling the well with images.

If you're feeling stuck or bored, remember that our characters are revealed through conflict. Give your hero a problem. Give him an antagonist. Give him obstacles to overcome. And give him a powerful want. Conflict reveals character—not exposition. We understand our characters as they are in relationship to the world.

Our story becomes more dynamic through working with the structure questions. We begin to see the universal truth at the heart of our story. It's like a kid who keeps asking "Why?" Children are not aware of limitations. They just figure that if there's something they don't know, it's because they haven't learned it yet.

"Why's the sun round?"

"Because there's a big fire at its center, and as it moves outward, it cools equally."

"Why?"

"Because heat cools at a standard rate."

"Why?"

"Uh . . . because . . ."

Children are endlessly curious. It can drive an adult crazy because we are confronted with how little we truly know, and how tenuous our existence is. A child can lead us to an existential crisis in three "Whys?"

Our job as writers is to be as curious as a child, to see things for the first time, and to never assume. We must always be willing to surrender our idea of the story to allow the larger story to emerge. We are seeking to understand the nature of things, the underlying forces at work.

If we're writing a memoir, we have an *idea* of our story because we lived it. However, our idea of our story is not the whole story. Story is not simply about what happened, it's about the meaning we ascribe to what happened. The challenge in memoir is to avoid becoming so attached to our story that we lose sight of why we are compelled to tell it. It's like the difference between journaling and storytelling. Journaling is personal while stories are universal. A certain objective detachment is valuable in writing memoir as it allows for greater specificity. When we see ourselves as *the hero*, we tend to have greater objectivity. Writing is primal rather than emotional. An objective detachment allows us to be connected more fully to the primal.

As we imagine the world of our story, we are putting our characters into situations that may cause us to question old beliefs. Through this process we are often forcing ourselves to explore the nature of dynamics we may have otherwise overlooked. This can be exhilarating, but also very tiring. We must be gentle with ourselves as we plow forward, and we must be conscious of this phenomenon lest we make meaning out of it. Fatigue, self-doubt, confusion: these are not indications that our project should be abandoned. We must keep exploring. The exhaustion is temporary.

Having fun on the page requires a lot of energy. Have you ever noticed how much sleep a kid needs. I advocate naps. Your subconscious will reward you for it.

WRITING EXERCISES FOR TODAY:

As your hero, write for five minutes . . .

1. "The bravest thing I've ever done . . ."

2. "The most cowardly thing I've ever done. . ."

Until tomorrow,
Al

DAY 6

"A creation of importance can only be produced when its author isolates himself. It is a child of solitude."
—JOHANN WOLFGANG VON GOETHE

THE STRUCTURE QUESTIONS

Hi Writers,

I encourage *imagining the world of your story longhand.* If your handwriting is illegible, that's OK. Personally, I rarely go back and read what I've written. Something weird happens when I write it down. I become connected to my story and tend to remember the essence or key images that I've scribbled down. Remember that we are not writing prose! We are simply panning for gold.

At this point, try writing a one- or two-paragraph synopsis of your story. It could be as general as boy meets girl, boy loses girl, boy gets girl. We are after the most general sense of a beginning, a middle and an end. It's not necessary to have the entire story worked out. As a matter of fact, it's important at this stage that we hold all of the images loosely as the story is revealed to us. The most important thing is that we maintain an aliveness in our characters, a sense of surprise and danger about what they might do next, while allowing for the most rudimentary sense of a journey to reveal itself. Will this journey look different a week from now? Yes. But that's OK, because we are holding it all loosely.

The structure questions speak to the largest turning points

in our hero's journey. Much like the five stages of grief identified by Elizabeth Kubler-Ross, some key universal stages exist in our hero's journey toward a shift in perception. The structure questions are not to be answered definitively so much as they are a tool to guide us toward a more dynamic vision of our story. Gradually we may notice a plot revealing itself. This plot is the vehicle that carries our hero through to his shift in perception.

As we continue to explore the world of our story, we can ask ourselves:

- Do I have a sense of what my hero wants?

- Do I have a sense of my hero's transformation?

- Do I have an image of what my hero surrenders?

- How does my hero reframe what he wants?

If I attempted to answer these questions at this stage and understand them intellectually, I would get very depressed and want to throw the whole thing away. Our story exists beyond our intellect; it is visceral—it lives in our body. The desire to write is connected to the desire to evolve. We are channels. Something wants to be written through us and we are uniquely qualified to write it. We are not looking for answers. We are allowing ourselves to be steered toward a greater truth through a series of events to which our hero responds.

WRITING EXERCISES FOR TODAY:

Choose an antagonist in your story and as this character, write for five minutes . . .

1. "What brings me joy is . . ."

2. "What breaks my heart is . . ."

3. "What makes me angry is . . ."

Now do the same for your protagonist.

Until tomorrow,
Al

DAY 7

"There are three rules for writing. Unfortunately, no one can agree what they are."

—W. SOMERSET MAUGHAM

THERE ARE NO RULES

Hi Writers,

Sometimes we want rules because we think they will make us safe or keep us on track. They won't. The artist's job is to shine a light on the truth. We are uncovering hypocrisy, upending the status quo, and shedding convention. Even the structure questions are not rules—they are just questions!

Some of us may not be writing a *traditionally structured* novel. We may be writing a series of short stories or essays with a central character, or the content may be in the form of journal entries or blogs, or perhaps it's a book of short stories with no central character but rather a theme that is being explored through a variety of characters. If we don't take the structure questions too literally, they can provide an opportunity to stretch our imaginations, to invite up images that make our work more dynamic.

We are uniquely qualified to tell our story. Everything we need to know to resolve the dilemma at the heart of our story lies within. Our job is to maintain a spirit of curiosity. The hero's journey is often the journey out of victimhood, and so this process often involves the reframing of an old idea.

Remember that story structure is not a formula.

We are simply inquiring into the world of our story to allow compelling circumstances to emerge. Everything we imagine either belongs in our story or is leading us to what ultimately belongs. We can't do this wrong.

WRITING EXERCISE FOR TODAY:

Write for ten minutes, imagining your hero transformed at the end of the story.

- How is he relating differently to other characters as the result of his journey?

- What has he come to understand?

- What new choice does he make?

This exercise can reveal a goldmine of images for what precedes our ending. For example: If our hero is willing to forgive someone at the end of the story, we might be curious about a moment in the story in which he is absolutely unwilling to forgive. If he is laughing at the end, at what point in the story did he weep? This exercise can help us clarify our hero's character arc. The more dynamic it is, the more compelling the story.

This is a great exercise to return to. It will provide an increasingly specific relationship to our ending. It's helpful to have a sense of the ending so that we can put our hero in real jeopardy and know that it is temporary.

Until tomorrow,
Al

WEEK 2

STORY STRUCTURE

While continuing to imagine the world of the story, this week we begin to outline. We don't figure out our story, but rather allow an outline to emerge through inquiring into the structure questions. This week is about developing a sense of the story as we move from a general to a more specific relationship to the story. Our relationship to the story will shift and grow. The key this week is to *hold it all loosely.*

DAY 8

"Nothing is more desirable than to be released from an affliction, but nothing is more frightening than to be divested of a crutch."   —JAMES BALDWIN

THE DILEMMA AT THE HEART OF OUR STORY

Hi Writers,

As we head into week two, let's remember that we are doing this because it is fun! If the structure questions are getting us down, we can toss them in the garbage . . . but just for today. (We may want to fish them out first thing in the morning.) The most important thing is that our characters live. Let's stay connected to the madness, to that wild impulse that screams, "I have something to say!"

When we get scared or confused, we need to come back to this impulse. If we are feeling bored, we allow it to stir us. We can't solve our hero's problem in our heads. We just need to imagine him transformed at the end of the story. As we imagine, we are provided with all sorts of ideas and images that precede the ending.

In my novel *Diamond Dogs*, the hero, Neil, accidentally kills a schoolmate on the highway. When I first imagined the world of the story I had only that one fact. As I continued to inquire, I wondered how the story ended. I didn't try to figure out the ending, but rather, imagined a sense of my hero at the end of the story. How was he relating differently to his father? What had he come to understand as a result of his journey? How was the dilemma resolved?

What was the visual metaphor, the image that captured the essence of the story at the end?

As I pondered these questions, ideas came to me, and I realized that they were a goldmine of images for what preceded the ending.

Imagining our hero transformed is a sure way to gain insight into our ending, while eliciting images and ideas for what precedes it. We are not after a concrete series of events, but rather a sense of how the hero has been altered by the end. This sense leads us, in time, to that concrete series of events. Of course, the story never unfolds exactly as we had imagined. If it did, there would be no reason to write it.

If our hero is at peace at the end, be curious about where he is not at peace in the story. If he's willing to share intimacies at the end, be curious about the secrets he is keeping within the story. This gives him a dramatic arc. It gives him somewhere to go.

Let's be willing to drop our preconceived notion of our story and be curious about our story at its core. Is it about love, revenge, truth, freedom, justice, hope, passion, identity, redemption, charity? As we inquire into the nature of our hero's dilemma, images begin to appear, and very gradually a semblance of a story begins to reveal itself.

THE HERO'S JOURNEY: THE THREE-ACT STORY STRUCTURE

This is a basic overview and brief explanation of story structure. It is the fundamental paradigm for the hero's journey, from innocence to wisdom. The hero wants something. The stakes are life and death. Always. What he wants is connected to an idea of what it will provide for him: "I want love because then it will complete me." (Notice how the seed of defeat is built right into the hero's idea of what he wants.) Be curious about tracking your hero's goal through each one of the major plot points. And once again, hold all of this loosely. We are exploring structure as an invitation to make our story more dynamic. Stories take many forms. All are valid.

You might find it helpful to outline the story on three sheets of paper, with each sheet delineating an act.

ACT ONE

OPENING: Our novel begins on page one by establishing the world of our story. We are also introducing tension. Something is unresolved in this world.

DILEMMA: There is a dilemma at the heart of every story. This is different from a problem. It is the core struggle around which every character in the story revolves. Some people call this the theme or the dramatic question. It is personal to the hero yet universally relatable to the reader.

INCITING INCIDENT: Something happens that sets our story in motion. Our hero responds or reacts.

OPPOSING ARGUMENT: How does my antagonist respond to the hero? It is important in Act One to illustrate for our reader, through action, the specific challenge our hero faces in achieving his goal.

END OF ACT ONE: We have likely met most of the main characters. We have set up the story. The hero makes a decision that he can't go back on. Reluctance often precedes this decision, until it becomes apparent that he must take this journey.

ACT TWO

FALSE VICTORY: The hero glimpses the possibility of achieving his goal. There is an identifiable shift in our hero, a distinct growth from the beginning of the story. This is often a moment of false hope for the hero.

MIDPOINT OF ACT TWO: There is no going back. This moment often occurs as the result of an event or some new information that forces the hero to respond. It often involves a moment of temptation as our hero measures his desire against the potential cost of achieving his goal.

HERO SUFFERS: Our hero begins to understand the difficulty of what he has signed up for. He begins to stagger under the weight of the conflict.

END OF ACT TWO: The hero surrenders his idea of what he wants. He recognizes that getting it is impossible. He surrenders because he has no choice. This is the moment that the hero may become conscious, for the first time, of the nature of his dilemma. It is the death of his old identity. It is out of this death that he rises from the ashes by reframing his relationship to his goal.

ACT THREE

In Act Three, the hero accepts the reality of his situation, and although he has surrendered his want, this does not mean he gives it up. For example, we don't ever stop wanting love, but we might recognize that our idea that someone else could complete us through loving us has set us on a path of self-destruction and despair.

BATTLE SCENE: The hero makes a new choice. He is awake to the dilemma. It is a battle between the want and the need. The battle is internal though it often manifests itself externally. Oftentimes, this is where it becomes possible for the hero to get what he wants, if what he wants belongs in his life. Sometimes he may be offered what he wants only to realize that he has found something much more valuable to him.

NEW EQUILIBRIUM: Our hero is returned home. The dilemma is resolved.

THIS WEEK

We have been inquiring into the structure questions and perhaps some images have been coming up. Now we are going to get a sense of what the story wants to be.

Get three sheets of paper. On page one, write the Act One plot points, page two the Act Two plot points, and page three the Act Three points. Of course, you are not expected to have your story *worked out* at this point, but be curious about what images come up and start to get a sense of what these major story beats might be. This way you can see your story on three manageable pieces of paper. Write the scenes and images that come to you in point form. Be very brief. Put them down in a loose order. Sit quietly with these three pages and with a separate notebook, continue to imagine the world of your story, scribbling down scenes, images, etc. and then put the scenes in point form on one of the three pages. As you do this, over time a story will begin to be revealed to you.

And remember our mantras:

- I am not writing my story yet. I am just exploring the world.

- I give myself permission to write poorly.

- I give myself permission to write whatever wants to be written through me, even if it seems at odds with my idea of the story.

- I give myself permission to never show my story to anyone.

WRITING EXERCISES FOR TODAY:

1. Write for five minutes: "The dilemma at the heart of my story is . . ."

2. As your hero, write for five minutes: "My relationship to God is . . ."

Until tomorrow,
Al

WEEK 2: THOUGHTS AND REMINDERS

- The desire to write is connected to the desire to evolve.

- Why is this day unlike any other? Be curious about the nature of what is happening, as opposed to the initial idea of the inciting incident. It is not that our idea is wrong, but as we explore the nature, we may discover a more specific relationship between the hero's goal and the incident.

- As we inquire into the structure questions, we hold our story loosely. If we are flexible, our story will lead us where it wants to go.

- Our hero's goal never wavers; however, his approach to getting it is always changing.

- Our hero's goal is always connected to an idea of what it will mean when he achieves it.

- Our hero's goal or want is the beating heart of the story. It is directly connected to the various plot points.

HOMEWORK FOR THE WEEK

1. Continue imagining the world of the story, i.e. free writing. If you get tired or bored, write from the stream-of-consciousness exercises near the back of the book.

2. Continue inquiring into the structure questions. Begin a point form outline of your story on three sheets of paper. Hold the images loosely. Stay curious.

DAY 9

"To gain your own voice, forget about having it heard. Become a saint of your own province and your own consciousness." —**Allen Ginsberg**

HOLDING OUR IDEA LOOSELY

Hi Writers,

If we ever feel like we are writing in circles, we might be trapped by our idea of the story. Sometimes we can cling so tightly to our premise that we are unable to step back and inquire into the nature of what we're trying to express. We may be fearful that if we let go of our idea of the story everything will collapse. The only thing that will collapse is our idea. This might seem scary at first, but let's consider taking the risk.

Sometimes we convince ourselves that we know the way the story goes. What if we got excited about not knowing? The possibilities become endless. This is a process. It's a war of attrition as we inch our way into the unknown. We can get excited every time we imagine a new and interesting way to nudge our hero toward greater jeopardy.

For the next eighty-one days, let's see what happens when we allow ourselves to stay out of the result. We cannot make a mistake. It isn't possible. We are simply investigating the possibilities that enter our imagination. We listen to our characters and imagine them in relationship to each other. We inquire further and we write it down. We don't have to understand what we write. That comes later.

Let's be willing to write the forbidden. Let's be surprised by our characters and trust that the story lives fully within us. Remember that story builds on itself. Each stage in our story happens as a result of what happened previously. Our hero is always making decisions in the hopes of getting what he wants. Let's continue to investigate what happens as our hero advances in the face of worthy antagonists. Story is alchemy. It is through the opposing forces that our hero is brought to his surrender, and finally transformed.

WRITING EXERCISES FOR TODAY:

As your hero, write for five minutes:

1. "My greatest accomplishment has been . . ."

2. "My greatest regret has been . . ."

Until tomorrow,
Al

DAY 10

"The end of our exploring will be to arrive where we started and know the place for the first time."
—T.S. ELIOT

THE HERO TAKES ACTION

Hi Writers,

As we imagine the world of our story, we might consider the moments following our hero's surrender at the end of Act Two. The end of Act Two is like a coin with two sides. On one side is surrender as the hero recognizes the impossibility of ever getting what he wants, while on the other side is the realization that what he thought would make his life unimaginable did not, in fact, destroy him. Perhaps a new possibility appeared as a result of this defeat.

Perhaps we have had the experience of trying hard to make a relationship work only to have it fall apart. We are standing there, lost and bereft, wondering what happened, and even terrified that it might happen again. And what if we reached that place where we said, "I don't know how to do this. This is impossible for me to figure out."

When we surrender our idea that we are supposed to know how to do something, we tend to relax and sometimes even have a sense of humor about the situation. When we realize that we are not in control, our perspective widens and new possibilities emerge. We begin to glimpse the true nature of the situation. Ironically, it is from this place of not knowing that we become willing to explore avenues we might previously have been resistant to because we were so busy forcing our idea of what we wanted into action.

In Act Three, the hero might take an action that rises directly out of this new awareness. It might be "I can't figure this out, so why don't I at least enjoy myself?" The action could be that our hero finally takes the tango classes he has been putting off, or he takes a writing workshop and writes the novel he has always wanted to get on the page. It is through taking this action, simply for its own sake, that a shift occurs. It becomes possible for him to get what he wants if what he wants belongs in his life.

This is what it means to *reframe our hero's want*. Our hero still wants love but not at the expense of betraying himself. In accepting the reality of his situation, he takes actions that reap benefits.

THE NATURE OF OUR STORY VERSUS OUR IDEA OF OUR STORY

Our *idea* is a limited version of reality that carries with it all our subconscious baggage and preconceptions. When the smoke clears, we are left with the true nature of the situation. Let's say John breaks up with Susie, and Susie wonders what is wrong with her. (That would be an idea, right? "There must be something wrong with me that he would break up with me.") However, the nature of the situation may actually be that John is already married.

Our idea is limited by our perception of ourselves and the world. The nature of the situation lives beyond our ego and our fears. It is only in surrendering our idea of the way we believe things ought to be that we begin to glimpse the nature of the ways things actually are.

WRITING EXERCISES FOR TODAY:

As your hero, write for five minutes:

1. "I believe my role in life is to . . ."

2. "My favorite thing to do is . . ."

Until tomorrow,
Al

DAY 11

*"Curiosity about life in all of its aspects, I think, is still
the secret of great creative people."*
　　　　　　　　　　　　　　　　—LEO BURNETT

WHAT IS MY STORY ABOUT?

Hi Writers,

We have good days and bad days. One day we love the direction of
our story, and the next we're riddled with self-doubt. This is just
part of the process. We come back to our original impulse and inquire into the world of our story. This process is akin to running a
marathon. We're logging miles on the page. Some days our imagination is on fire, while other days feel like a slog.

- Let go of the result.

- Continue to inquire.

- Hold it loosely.

- Be willing to let go of your fixed idea of the story,
  in order to glimpse the larger picture.

　　All of our ideas are in service of that thing we want to express. What is our story about? Let's remain open to all of the different ways in which our characters might go in directions we may
not have anticipated.

　　Although we may have a very clear sense of our story's location, timeframe and premise, if we follow the principle of *holding it loosely*, we realize that we are always willing to drop an idea, any idea, and explore another if we sense it is going to bring us to a more powerful expression of our story. If it doesn't seem to work, we can always go back to our original idea.

Being certain about any aspect of our story limits us. Let's trust that the story lives fully within us, and that something valid wants to be expressed. There's an experience far more empowering than certainty, and that is a faith in the fundamental truth of our story, a growing belief that it is not necessary to force anything, but rather to inquire into the nature of what we want to express. Just as water dumped on a concrete surface reaches every pore, a relaxed and curious mind naturally explores the world, searching for the most compelling way to express the story. Our subconscious is forever trying to make order out of chaos. We must trust it. As we allow our character's lives to become increasingly complicated, our subconscious is searching to find a new order.

Certainty can suffocate the truth before it's brought to life. The opposite of certainty isn't uncertainty, but rather a connection to the infinite possibilities for our story.

BACKSTORY

The world of our story includes a backstory. If we're feeling stuck, let's remember that our characters have a past. They don't begin on page one, tabula rasa. Their past informs their present. It's vital to explore our characters in order to fully understand how they got to this place.

WRITING EXERCISES FOR TODAY:

As your hero, write for five minutes . . .

1. "My childhood dream was to . . ."

2. "My perfect day would be . . ."

Now do this as an antagonist in your story.

Until tomorrow,
Al

DAY 12

"Once freedom lights its beacon in a man's heart, the gods are powerless against him."

— JEAN-PAUL SARTRE

FREEDOM

Hi Writers,

Many of us are writing stories of freedom, but struggle to imagine what that might look like for our hero. What if we simply imagined our hero at the end of the story? What sense do we have of him in relationship to other characters? *In relationship* might mean they are no longer speaking to each other, or maybe that he's come to accept another character in a different way and in doing so has found some peace. Perhaps our hero has learned something about himself, and in doing so, finds his tribe. Be curious about how the dilemma is resolved. Our hero is liberated by reframing his relationship to his unattainable desire.

It's easier to imagine freedom for others than for ourselves because there is often a high cost for freedom. It often involves the betrayal of a lie. Stories often begin with a hero's false belief, from the swan in *The Ugly Duckling*, to Nora in *A Doll's House*. I use the word betrayal because there is something psychically violent that happens when our hero surrenders his old identity. By recognizing that his desire was in fact, standing in the way of him ever getting what he wants, he experiences a death. And in reframing his relationship to this desire, he betrays the old system.

Our hero never stops wanting, but he begins to see what he wants in a different light. The swan still wants to belong, but it is only in recognizing the impossibility of ever belonging with the ducks that she can find the other swans. Freedom might be the willingness to choose one's dreams over some idea of security. It might mean defying an old idea shared by the group. Our job as writers is to remain curious and to track the beats in a specific and believable way that leads to a transformation. We do this by trusting our gut, and by having a sense of where our hero lands in the end. There can be great value in imagining our hero at the end of the story. When we have confidence in our destination we are more inclined to put our hero in jeopardy.

WRITING EXERCISES FOR TODAY:

As your hero, write for five minutes . . .

1. "The lie I continually tell myself is . . ."

2. "I fear that when people look at me, they see . . ."

Until tomorrow,
Al

DAY 13

"The value of identity of course is that so often with it comes purpose."   —RICHARD R. GRANT

NEW IDEAS/FEAR/MULTIPLE PROTAGONISTS

Hi Writers,

We may discover as we write that new story ideas are beginning to emerge. This is very common. The channel is opening up. Sometimes we get excited by these new ideas and want to discard what we are currently working on. If we have a pattern of not finishing what we start, this is likely resistance. So when the floodgates open and new stories start pouring in, it's time to get a filing cabinet so these ideas don't take up space in our brain.

Sometimes we resist the conflict in our story because it scares us or feels forbidden. Remember that the desire to write is connected to the desire to evolve. Therefore our story asks everything of us because if it didn't, we would never surrender our old identity. The old identity must die for a new one to emerge. Those areas that scare us are leading us to freedom, but first our hero must experience the death of his old self. If we continue to inquire, and hold the images loosely, a narrative gradually reveals itself.

Let's imagine that our hero is ambitious and wants to be famous, to make his mark in the world. He has made meaning out of this goal, such as "When I am famous, I will be loved," or "I will feel important," or "I will have arrived." Perhaps the hero achieves some notoriety and it becomes clear that his idea of public recognition, in and of itself, does not translate to feeling any differently, and may, in fact, lead to a compulsive desire to chase after more fame in an attempt to feel better about himself. Our hero has invested his identity in this pursuit only to discover that not only is it wrongheaded, but in fact his blind pursuit of this goal has actually steered him away from all that he actually wanted, namely to be connected to himself and others.

Or perhaps we have a hero who wants to be famous and he never achieves public recognition on the level he had hoped. Eventually he understands that it is never going to happen. Perhaps he wanted to play center in the NBA and worked hard, but at some point it became apparent that his window of opportunity had closed. He is devastated. His identity was forged squarely on this goal. Now what? This is his moment of surrender. Perhaps he feels as if life isn't worth living anymore. Perhaps he suddenly realizes that the *meaning* he had made out of this goal, that he could provide a better life for his family, was not, in fact, the whole truth. Is the family's future dependent on our hero making it to the NBA? It's doubtful, though he may be convinced of it at the time. We surrender when we run out of choices. His old idea, that his family's future was dependent on him playing center in the NBA, was incorrect. He may discover that all of the hard work and sacrifices he made have left him with the skills necessary to function at a high level in another area of his choosing. With this new awareness, he can take action, not toward his former goal (that he would be the world's first 5′4″ center), but toward his true goal of helping his family. His journey was not a waste. It armed him with the skills necessary to proceed. Surrender is the crucial point in a story that precedes a transformation.

As we write, doubts and fears will almost certainly arise. We don't have to ignore our feelings. In fact, we can use them. We ask ourselves, "Where does this feeling or situation live in the world of my story?" We can use everything: our fears, our doubts, our joy and our grief.

If it all feels too intense, we can pay a visit to our hero transformed and ask ourselves what our hero's life looks like at the end of the story. When we remember that there is a reason for this journey, we're more inclined to investigate those areas that scare us.

We don't inquire into structure to limit our imagination, but rather to set it free. When we use the term *hero*, we can hold it loosely. It may mean an antihero, a character marginalized by society, or it could mean a protagonist. Although oftentimes a story is told through the eyes of one protagonist and follows the hero's journey in a formal way, story structure is by no means a formula. It's a paradigm for transformation. There is nothing we can imagine that cannot be contained in our story. Story structure invites our subconscious to organize a host of disparate ideas into a coherent narrative that leads to a transformation. We are seeking to imagine a story that becomes bigger than we are, where we can step back with wonder and say, "Where did that come from?"

In Gabriel Garcia Marquez's novel *One Hundred Years of Solitude*, there is no single protagonist. As this epic rolls along we meet, one after another, the members and offspring of the Buendia clan over the course of a century. However, as we look closely we begin to recognize patterns, a whole underlying world, and we see that these stories express a theme. The story begins, "Many years later, as he faced the firing squad, Colonel Aureliano Buendia was to remember that distant afternoon when his father took him to discover ice." Through Aureliano's eyes, we enter into his world, the magical town of Macondo. The story begins with an incident that doesn't happen until much later in the book, but we are hooked. We must know what happened to Aureliano that led him to this moment.

Marquez had a vision to tell the story of a family over a hundred years. Perhaps he wondered, "How on earth do I find a way into this story? What could possibly be the single defining event to begin this epic journey?" He could have just begun with the second sentence and described Aureliano running along the riverbed's polished stones *like prehistoric eggs*. But the opening sentence creates narrative drive. It provides tension and acts as a framing device to take us into the story.

Russell Bank's novel *The Sweet Hereafter* is also narrated by multiple protagonists. One might describe the story in this way: "It begins with a school bus accident. The bus rolls into a near-frozen lake and sinks. The town is submerged in grief. A lawyer comes to town to investigate and offer his services. A man is having an affair with a woman, and through the story his relationship alters. The high school beauty queen, crippled by the accident, confronts her abuser."

It is *traditionally* structured while told from the point of view of four protagonists. There is an inciting incident (the bus crash). A decision is made (lawyer arrives in town to profit from the tragedy) that forces the town to relive the experience. A surrender takes place as the lawyer experiences the disintegration of his bond with his son and finally, the young girl confronts her abuser (battle scene) as a result of her shift in perception.

It is a story that seems to break all of the rules until we realize that there are no rules. The author has supplied us with an inciting incident, a decision, a surrender and a transformation. These key points seem to be intrinsic to most stories, yet where and how they appear are entirely up to the author. Perhaps the only rule is that we not bore our reader.

It is more important to inquire into the structure questions and allow images to emerge than it is to force our ideas into a formula. Our story's structure might not look the way we think it should. The truth is that we probably have an innate sense of structure already from all of the books and movies we have read and seen. The story structure questions are an invitation to allow our story to be the most dynamic experience possible. It's more important that our story live than that we follow our idea of some rule.

WRITING EXERCISES FOR TODAY:

1. As your hero, write for five minutes . . . "Something I know that no one else knows is . . ."

2. Write a five-minute stream-of-consciousness dialogue between your hero and an antagonist. Be curious about what they want and the obstacles that stand in the way of achieving this.

Until tomorrow,
Al

DAY 14

"When we are not sure, we are alive."

—GRAHAM GREENE

GOING DEEPER

Hi Writers,

At this stage we are less concerned with making our story work, and more concerned with remaining engaged to the aliveness of our characters. Let's see them in conflict. Let's allow this conflict to build, even if we feel we are being led into uncharted territory. Writing is an act of faith. We trust our subconscious to reveal the story to us. This may seem abstract and can even feel frustrating at times, but then we have another breakthrough and are taken to a deeper and more specific understanding of our story. This process is about going from the general to the specific. We're getting a sense of our characters, what they want and how they relate to each other, and from this place we begin to descend into the minutiae of their lives.

We are like deep-sea divers, submerging slowly into the world of our stories. It takes time to get our bearings as we go deeper. We might discover, "My God, I had no idea my characters were so crazed, so passionate, so shut down, so in denial, so sweet, so cruel, so complicated!" It can feel strange as we adjust to this new place. Our story seems different. Things are happening that we didn't expect. As we listen to our subconscious and allow images to emerge, our story tells us what it wants to be.

At this point, if you absolutely feel like writing passages of prose, then go for it. This is your process. There are no rules.

Lastly, let's give ourselves permission to write poorly. We have a tendency to be so result-oriented that we never allow ourselves time to grow and to make mistakes. Why we write is far more important than what we write. If we are writing to make a million dollars or prove something to our parents, we might run out of gas before reaching our goal. Let the thrill of creation be its own reward.

WRITING EXERCISES FOR TODAY:

Write for five minutes…

1. "The secret my hero won't tell anyone is . . ."

2. "The secret my hero won't tell himself is . . ."

Hint: The secret our hero won't tell others is usually something he is ashamed of or that he believes might weaken his position. The secret he doesn't tell himself is that he is fundamentally okay, and if he understood this he might not need to be doing that thing he's doing that is creating conflict.

Now choose an antagonist and repeat the exercises.

Until tomorrow,
Al

WEEK 3

NARRATIVE DRIVE

We continue to outline this week, developing a more specific relationship to our story. We explore our hero's wants and needs and the worthy antagonists who propel him forward. Our hero's goal is the throughline that drives the narrative.

DAY 15

"First, find out what your hero wants, then just fol-low him!"   **—RAY BRADBURY**

PLOT POINTS

Hi Writers,

Let's write down everything we know about our story and then step back and see what our imagination has come up with in two short weeks. Not too shabby.

This is the beginning of our story. Are there holes? Hell, yeah. And there will be holes when we start writing our first draft. Are we seeing a beginning, a middle, and an end, even if just glimpses? Does our hero have a problem that is impossible to solve? Every story has at its heart a dilemma, a problem that cannot be solved without creating another problem. Without a dilemma, there can be no surrender, and without a surrender, there can be no transformation.

If we're having trouble identifying the dilemma, it doesn't mean that there isn't one. We just seek out the tension that plagues our hero. This is where the dilemma lies. The dilemma is resolved by reframing our hero's relationship to what he wants.

Let's say our hero is the son of a great mountain climber. He wants to climb Mount Everest because he believes he will finally receive his father's approval. His dilemma might be that he resents his father for not accepting him as he is (his true passion is competitive origami), and so, even if he does climb Everest and his father tells him how proud he is, it might only reinforce his despair that he will never be accepted as a first-rate competitive origami-ist.

So how might this idea get reframed? Well, first let's remember that we don't surrender until we have run out of choices. Perhaps our hero climbs Everest, and his father finally gives him that hug he's been waiting for, and the son still feels empty. At this point he may experience great despair, and in his despair, he may recognize that the idea that his father must validate his existence in order for his life to have meaning is, in fact, the source of his pain. In having this awareness, he reframes his want. Does he still want validation from Dad? Yup. Our hero's want doesn't go away. Ever. But he understands that making his self-worth conditional on this desire is putting his life on hold.

And so, perhaps he decides to validate himself by entering the world of origami competitions where he'll attempt to create the holy grail of paper animals by constructing a porcupine with a postage stamp. By becoming true to himself, the validation he desired from his father, though welcome, is not crucial, and as a result it opens a door for the father to finally express his approval and for the son to be able to accept it. Or the father may be a narcissist who can only see his own reflection, in which case the son can finally understand and accept his old man's limitations.

Knowing what our hero wants can be tricky. What our hero wants is connected to an idea of what it will give him. Isn't this true in our own lives? "I want love, success, peace, validation, a promotion, freedom, etc. because I believe that when I get this it will mean something. Then I'll be happy. Then I'll feel okay about myself. Then I'll know I've arrived."

Let's continue to inquire into the nature of what our hero wants. It's not enough to say, "My hero wants his mother." We must be specific. For example: "My hero wants his mother so he can know who he is." The want is primal. The stakes are life and death. And then we allow our imaginations to wander and images and ideas emerge to create a scenario through which we can explore the question of "Do I need my mother in order to know who I am?"

Writers often ask me questions like, "Should my hero decide to break the four-minute mile at this point in the story, or later?" as if I can answer that.

Rather than trying to figure out when Roger decides to run the four-minute mile, think of it like this: The plot point is not determined by what happens, but by what happens as related to the theme, meaning that *a man deciding to break the four-minute mile* could be an inciting incident, a decision at end of the first act, and even an act of surrender at end of Act Two. However, without context, the event is irrelevant. Our theme ascribes meaning to the event. Roger's decision to break the world record exists as a means of exploring a universal truth. For now, it's enough to simply have a sense that the image or situation holds something for us. If we're allowing an outline to emerge, we can place the scene where we sense it belongs, and as we work with our outline, it might become apparent that it belongs somewhere else.

Remember that our hero's want never changes. However, his relationship to what he wants is always changing. For example: Bill wants love and so he asks Sue out. Later, Bill and Sue get married. And then, perhaps, he isn't happy with his idea of how she is loving him and so he divorces her. He takes all of these actions in pursuit of the same goal: love.

BOREDOM IS RESISTANCE

If we feel bored doing these writing exercises and find ourselves writing the same thing over and over again... Stop! We may not be connected to the process. It can't be possible at this point to have inquired completely into the world of our story. Each question begets more questions. What do our characters want to tell us? What happens next? Let's put our hero in jeopardy and keep him there!

Boredom is sometimes a symptom of fear. We may be afraid to go deeper into our story because of what may arise. If we truly investigate the nature of our story, ideas and images are going to emerge that challenge us. Questions might be raised that threaten our preconceived notions. This is fantastic! Our story is getting juicy.

There's an adage: *Write what you know.* In fact, I think we are drawn to write what we believe in order to gain a fundamental knowing. We are drawn to the ideas and images in our story because they contain for us the seed of something that will challenge our old ideas.

If we're feeling bored, let's get out of the result. We can let go of the idea that writing this book will save our life, make us richer, younger, and more desirable. It is impossible not to, at times, fantasize about the result or worry about whether or not we might be wasting our time. This is garden-variety resistance and though it may come up frequently (and even be convincing), it's of little use.

The solution is simple. We must be more curious about our story than we are about the result. We tend to worry that we can't do it, that we will fail, that we are not educated enough, or talented enough, when the truth is that we are just scared. When we get out of the result, this process may start to become fun.

WRITING EXERCISES FOR TODAY:

As your hero, write for five minutes . . .

1. "My first love was . . ."

2. "The person I hate the most is . . ."

Now write this for an antagonist in your story.

Until tomorrow,
Al

WEEK 3: THOUGHTS AND REMINDERS

- There are no rules to novel writing. Our novel may have multiple protagonists, be a series of loosely connected short stories, be told in the second person, or be narrated by a sock puppet. Regardless, our job is to reflect the human experience, even if the story is about a bunch of animals on a farm.

- Story structure at its most basic involves three elements: Desire, surrender and transformation.

- Story structure is a way of holding our characters accountable to universal truths.

- The structure questions invite our subconscious to organize all of our disparate ideas into a coherent narrative without having to sacrifice anything essential.

- Whatever we feel strongly about is necessarily subjective, meaning that it has an opposing argument. When we frame what we feel strongly about as a statement, and become curious about the opposing arguments, a story begins to emerge.

- The desire to write is connected to the desire to evolve; therefore, as we explore the opposing argument, we are led to deeper truths about the fundamental conflict in our story.

- All of our characters revolve around a central dilemma.

- A transformation is simply a shift in perception.

- A transformation cannot occur without powerful opposition. Story is alchemy—we only transform through great pressure.

- Imagining our hero transformed invites up a goldmine of images for what precedes the climax of our story.

- The climax (or battle scene) is the moment in which our hero makes a new choice.

- Antagonists are not necessarily villains. An antagonist could be our hero's dearest friend.

- An antagonist is any character that stands in the way of the protagonist achieving his goal.

- We don't judge our characters. We inquire into the reasons for their choices.

- Our protagonist and antagonists all desire the same thing, though their approaches may differ wildly.

- It is through our hero's acceptance of the reality of his situation in Act Three that the dilemma is resolved.

- Let's be willing to explore possible blind alleys. We don't ever settle for our idea of our story. We explore the possibility of something beyond our idea even if it threatens to collapse our story. In doing so, we often discover new possibilities that may, in fact, reinforce what we are expressing.

HOMEWORK FOR THE WEEK

1. Write a three-page outline with a beginning, middle and end. Continue to imagine the world of your story, getting more specific with characters, scenes, and tracking your hero's want through the plot points.

2. Read *Diamond Dogs* and list the plot points, the hero's want and need, and the dilemma at the heart of the story. Day 22 contains a structural analysis/pop quiz of the book.

DAY 16

> "Write freely and as rapidly as possible and throw
> the whole thing on paper. Never correct or rewrite
> until the whole thing is down."
>
> —JOHN STEINBECK

THE PROCESS

Hi Writers,

In two weeks we start writing our first drafts. This means we have fourteen more days to imagine the world of our story and allow an outline to emerge. Don't fret if your storyline seems to be revealing itself slowly. Let's be more concerned about the dilemma at the heart of our story than our idea of where the story ought to go.

When I wrote my first novel *Diamond Dogs*, I had the idea that my hero, a high school senior, gets rid of the body. He accidentally kills a kid while driving late one night on the highway and he puts the body in the trunk. It seemed obvious to me that the only *logical* next thing for him to do would be to dispose of the body himself. But for some reason, it just didn't feel right. As I continued imagining the world of the story, I wondered 'What if his father was the local Sheriff? Wow, that would be a dilemma for Dad. And then, what if the father got rid of the body, and never talked about it to his son?!"

At that moment, the story cracked open for me. That single act defined for me the nature of the father/son relationship. The son would be relieved, but he would also look at his father with suspicion, setting into motion a quest for the hero to try and understand the truth of his mother's disappearance fourteen years earlier. Suddenly the story had layers that a moment earlier did not exist.

When the father disposes of the body, we understand the son's dilemma; if he comes clean, he will almost certainly go to prison, but if he doesn't, he will become like his father, a man emotionally cut off from the world. It is a problem that necessitates a shift in perception in order to be resolved.

Let's explore the mechanism that allowed for these revelations. First, I sensed that although logically it seemed obvious that the son would dispose of the body, something didn't feel right. It's easy to bullshit ourselves and try to force something that isn't working, but because I was *holding my story loosely*, even when I was fairly certain of the way I thought it should go, I was able to entertain another possibility.

Had I begun writing the story prior to this epiphany, the story might have gone off in some other direction. There is a rigor to this process, but it is not a *left-brain* kind of rigor. It's not quantifiable. The rigor is in continuing to allow ourselves to be entertained by the aliveness of our story, without ever locking it down. Eventually, as we continue to imagine, our character's actions will begin to suggest a plot and a coherent narrative will naturally emerge. Do we need to know every beat before we start writing? Absolutely not. And although there are no rules, it is often helpful to have a basic sense of the beginning, middle, and end before proceeding.

If you feel like the well is getting full, feel free to start doing *free writing* that you can use in the book. Everyone's process is different and I don't want you to feel hampered. However, I would encourage you to really use these next two weeks to continue imagining the world.

When we start our first drafts, we are going to spend roughly three weeks on the first act, five weeks on the second act, and the final week and six days on Act Three. This means that we want to think about the proportions of our story as we look at our outline. Again, no rules, but if we sense that a particular area is feeling vague or a little light, this may be a place to focus our curiosity.

We are getting more specific now. Again, we don't worry if our story has not completely revealed itself to us. The desire to write is the desire to evolve. If it had totally revealed itself, there would be no reason to write it.

WRITING EXERCISES FOR TODAY:

As your hero, write for five minutes . . .

1. "The defining moment of my life was when . . ."

2. "The one thing I could never survive would be . . ."

Now write this for an antagonist in your story.

Until tomorrow,
Al

DAY 17

"What is so wonderful about great literature is that it transforms the man who reads it towards the condition of the man who wrote, and brings to birth in us also the creative impulse."   —E. M. FORSTER

DESIRE

Hi Writers,

In keeping our stories dynamic through the desert of Act Two, we must explore the myriad ways our hero struggles to get what he wants. As we inquire into the nature of our hero's desire, it can seem fuzzy. As humans, we want many things. How on earth can we be expected to isolate one particular desire for our hero?

Whether we are conscious of it or not, our story sprang from a theme and is likely an investigation into a primal aspect of our common humanity, such as revenge, lust, justice, loyalty, fidelity, ambition, power, and freedom. Our hero's desire is connected to a theme. Getting specific about what our hero wants is not an intellectual process, but rather akin to a Polaroid photograph coming into focus. We have a sense of it, and as we continue to inquire, it begins to reveal itself more clearly in relation to the story that we are imagining.

Remember that our hero's desire is always connected to an idea of what he believes it will give him, e.g., "I want the promotion because it will give me security." When we are specific about the want, we can be specific about the ways in which our hero attempts to achieve his goal. And in turn, we can be curious about our antagonists' attempts to stand in his way. Upon examination, we notice that our hero and our antagonists desire the same thing. How they go about achieving their objectives can be very different. Oftentimes what separates our hero from our antagonist is a willingness to surrender his desire.

The hero of Ernest Hemingway's short story "The Short Happy Life of Francis Macomber," wants respect. He is on safari with his beautiful wife, hunting tigers in Africa. The story begins with Francis behaving cowardly. His wife is disgusted by him. That night, she leaves her tent to sleep with Wilson, their guide. The following morning, though emasculated, rather than withdrawing, Francis surrenders his pride and throws himself into the hunt. He hunts bravely, putting his life on the line. The tiger he has wounded races toward him. Facing death, he wins the respect of the hunters. His wife raises her rifle, ostensibly to shoot the tiger but instead, shoots her husband dead. She is unwilling to surrender her pride. Her desire to be respected has calcified into entitlement. Upon witnessing her husband's courage, she understands that her game is over. He will no longer tolerate her behavior. Rather than surrendering her pride, she takes his life.

The stakes are life and death for our characters. If our hero doesn't fulfill his desire, his life will be unimaginable. We must be willing to write the forbidden, to surprise ourselves with the depth of our hero's desire. There is nothing civilized about creating art. It's a rebellious act that paradoxically brings us closer to our fellow man.

WRITING EXERCISES FOR TODAY:

Every story begins with "Why is this day unlike any other?"

1. Write for five minutes, beginning with, "Today is the day. . ."

2. As your hero, write for five minutes, beginning with, "I have a habit of . . ."

Until tomorrow,
Al

DAY 18

"There's only one difference between published and unpublished writers and it is this—the first group see their work in print on the shelves of Waterstone's or Tesco or online at Amazon; the second group are yet to have physical evidence of the hours, weeks, years spent fashioning words into their patterns. You are already a writer."   **—Kate Mosse**

MORE ON DILEMMA

Hi Writers,

It's not necessary to define our hero's dilemma. Story isn't logical. It's more important to have a sense of the tension, to be curious about the nature of the dilemma and how it manifests through conflict. By exploring the nature of the dilemma, situations emerge that reveal story.

We know that we have a story when our hero's want is impossible to achieve. Our hero's want is connected to an idea of what it will give him. He attaches meaning to his goal such as, "When I get the promotion, everyone will respect me." Well, Joe may get the promotion, but only to discover he can't control who respects him. The impossible want was not the promotion, but the meaning he attached to it.

It's universal, isn't it? We attach meaning to something outside of ourselves. We strive for it and regardless of whether we succeed or fail, it never provides us with the lasting satisfaction we had hoped for. Inevitably we surrender our idea of what it should have meant. We reframe our goal. And as a result, it becomes possible to give ourselves what we need.

Remember, our hero's want never changes. It is consistent from beginning to end. It is the engine that drives the story. Its meaning may shift, and our hero's approach to achieving it may be constantly adjusting, but his desire never wavers. We never stop wanting approval, advancement, meaning, love, or connection.

By remaining connected to the dilemma we can stay on track in our process. The throughline lives in the dilemma. Sometimes we make decisions that don't raise the stakes. As our plot moves forward, it should also accumulate meaning. Within each scene, the tension builds, reaches critical mass, and then turns, leading the reader to a deeper understanding of the dilemma. The meaning rises directly out of the conflict between hero and antagonists, yet we must not mistake movement for actual conflict.

Sometimes we take detours. Our hero moves to Florida rather than confronting the antagonist. We think, "Well that's what I did in my life." What makes our hero heroic is the relentless pursuit of a goal. If our hero doesn't get what he wants, his life will be unimaginable. We must continually raise the stakes in order for our hero to surrender his old idea.

Writing a novel is a freefall. It demands that we have faith in something beyond our limited vision. Even as we know we are leading our hero to the gallows, we simply allow him to continue striving for his goal. He's led to the inevitable conclusion that what he wants is impossible to achieve based on his current identity. His current identity must be shed in order to wake him up to the reality of his situation. Only after this realization can he make choices that lead to something lasting.

We discover something greater than ourselves through inquiry. We begin to understand that through these series of images, we are actually seeking a resolution to a dilemma.

WRITING EXERCISES FOR TODAY:

As your hero, write for five minutes . . .

1. "The greatest thrill of my life was when . . ."

2. "My most painful memory is . . ."

Until tomorrow,
Al

DAY 19

*"The writer's only responsibility is to his art. He will
be completely ruthless if he is a good one. If a writer
has to rob his mother, he will not hesitate; the Ode
on a Grecian Urn is worth any number of old la-
dies."*   **—WILLIAM FAULKNER**

PERMISSION TO WRITE THE FORBIDDEN

Hi Writers,

As we approach the writing of our first draft, we may experience
a touch of fear. "Am I going to reveal my secrets? How vulnerable
should I allow myself to be?" Perhaps those silent agreements we
have maintained with our family and friends about the role we play
in these relationships are coming up for review. There is a ruthless-
ness to the creative act. It often involves a betrayal of the status quo.
If we are going to devote real time and energy to this endeavor, we
do not want to be working at cross-purposes. We must give ourselves permission to write the forbidden. I believe it is important
to write our first draft for ourselves. When we set ourselves free to
really let it rip, our writing crackles. It becomes dangerous and alive.

Permission might be a good word for the week as we continue to inquire more deeply.

This might sound dry but at heart, story is an argument. In
Judith Guest's novel *Ordinary People*, Calvin attempts to repair his
broken family after the death of his eldest son six months earlier. In

his attempt to realize this outcome, a rift widens between his wife and son. His dilemma has to do with the question of duty; as long as he feels responsible for their happiness, he can never find it for himself.

We can all relate to feeling that we ought to be able to control an outcome and our sense of frustration when we fail. Until Calvin considers himself, it is impossible to have a happy family because he realizes that he too is a member of this family.

It is likely that Judith Guest had at least a sense of the resolution as she set out to write her first draft. When we are armed with a basic sense of our ending, it connects us to our source, the place where all the images emerge. It also keeps us on track. In the first draft there can be a tendency to want to stray from the conflict. We may have a sense that we're losing control as our characters take on lives of their own. We may also seek to avoid conflict for fear of how we may be perceived. When we write the story for ourselves, we are more willing to take risks. We can get to the other side and realize that what we were betraying was a lie. Like Calvin in *Ordinary People*, we discover that we must consider ourselves. We discover that this is not selfishness, but rather our birthright.

This process might be scary, but no one ever died from inquiry . . . okay, there was Socrates.

WRITING EXERCISES FOR TODAY:

As your hero write for five minutes . . .

1. "The closest I ever came to murder was when . . ."

2. "When I want to comfort myself, I remember . . ."

Until tomorrow,
Al

DAY 20

"No artist is pleased. There is no satisfaction what-
ever at any time. There is only a queer, divine dis-
satisfaction, a blessed unrest that keeps us march-
ing and makes us more alive than others."
                                    —MARTHA GRAHAM

STORY INVOLVES A BETRAYAL

Hi Writers,

We begin flush with excitement, thrilled at the opportunity to express something in a way the world has never known. As we ven-
ture further into our story, the forest grows thick with ghosts from
our past. We become haunted by the ancient fear that we are not
up to the task. Surely we are destined to fail. We find ourselves,
consciously or not, in a duel with the beliefs of our ancestors. This
is inevitable, because story involves a betrayal. Inherent in every
transformation is the betrayal of a lie, an idea or belief that no longer serves our protagonist.

As writers we can become either paralyzed or thrilled by
this notion. The desire to write stems from the desire to evolve, to
untangle the lie we have been carrying around about ourselves. The
lie is that we are not enough, that we are not forgiven, that it is never
going to happen for us, that we should just forget it, pack up, and go
home.

Through story, we engage our subconscious in confronting

the meaning that our hero has attached to getting what he wants, only to discover that his desire has set up a situation that has guaranteed the impossibility of ever getting it. Our hero's mission is to surrender his old idea of himself so that a new one can be born.

This is challenging. It is courageous. It is something that no one out there will ever encourage us to do. The desire must come from within. It is the soft whisper at the edges of our consciousness. Our soul aches to know life in a way we can't grasp with our conscious mind. Writers are idealists. At our best, we are more interested in the nature of things than we are in our own particular struggle. Story is alchemy. If we trust the process and stick with it, our subconscious will tell us all we need to know.

WRITING EXERCISES FOR TODAY:

As your hero, write for five minutes . . .

1. "The greatest love of my life is . . ."

2. "The last time I remember laughing hard was when . . ."

Until tomorrow
Al

DAY 21

*"God has pitted you against a rough antagonist that
you may be a conqueror, and this cannot be without
toil."*   —EPICTETUS

ANTAGONISTS

Hi Writers,

Characters don't exist in a vacuum. Character is revealed through
conflict. If our story feels flat, let's give our hero a worthy antagonist. We understand our hero in relationship to others and his environment. His responses reveal his character. Don't worry about
making him likeable; just give him a powerful want. We will care
about him not because he is good but because he is human.

Antagonists are not necessarily bad. They are just characters who obstruct our hero's goal. There is a tension in every relationship, an awareness of consequence. For example, I may not
want to take out the garbage, but when I don't, well . . . my wife has
this look she gives me, and the cost of not taking it out is far greater
than just getting it done.

We can complicate this process when we get lost inside our
heads. Let's trust the story in our imagination, and when an image
or situation feels powerful, let's be curious about where it does belong rather than assuming we are doing it wrong. It's impossible to
make a mistake. Everything we imagine either belongs in our story
or is leading us to a more specific truth.

Our story is revealing itself. We're getting ready to write

our first drafts. We have one more week to imagine the world of our story and further clarify the outline, but if we have a sense of the beginning, the middle, and the end and a sense of the worthy antagonist, we may be ready to jump in and start writing. Although I personally recommend taking this time to really soak up the world so that in writing the first draft there is a deep well of images to draw from, this decision is up to you.

WRITING EXERCISES FOR TODAY:

As an antagonist in your story, write for five minutes . . .

1. "When I wake up, my first thought is . . ."

2. "My last thought before I fall asleep is . . ."

> Now do this for your hero.

HOMEWORK REMINDER:

For our structural analysis/pop quiz tomorrow on *Diamond Dogs*, please identify the following:
- The hero's want and need
- The dramatic question (dilemma)
- The inciting incident
- The opposing argument
- The hero's decision at the end of Act One
- The hero's false victory
- The hero is tempted
- The hero suffers
- The hero surrenders his goal
- The battle scene/hero makes a new choice
- New equilibrium

Until tomorrow,
Al

WEEK 4

GETTING MORE SPECIFIC

During this week we will continue to explore the world of the story and develop a specific outline. We may be getting itchy to begin writing our first draft (and we can start if we like). However, I suggest that we give ourselves one more week to develop a richer sense of the story. We will also do a story structure analysis of my novel *Diamond Dogs*.

DAY 22

"Even if my marriage is falling apart and my chil-
dren are unhappy, there is still a part of me that
says, 'God, this is fascinating!'"

—ERNEST HEMINGWAY

INQUIRY

Hi Writers,

If an event in our outline seems out of place, we may want to be curious about why we wrote it down. What are we trying to express?
At the heart of every story, a universal human condition is being
explored.

Denis Johnson's *Jesus' Son* is a series of nine loosely connected stories about a drug addict. They are humorous, horrify-
ing, and heartbreaking. As compelling as each story is, the whole is
greater than the sum of its parts. The meaning deepens with each
story and leads the reader to a greater understanding of the hero.
Ultimately, it's a story of hope.

If one is going to investigate the nature of hope, why not explore it through the most hopeless case imaginable? If the nameless
hero in *Jesus' Son* can find hope, then perhaps there is hope for all
of us. The protagonist is a man marginalized by the ravages of his
addiction. As the story progresses, a man of poetry and humor is
revealed. In spite of ourselves, we care for him. We become invested, and as we reach the final story, in which he blunders into rehab

and experiences an awareness of another's pain for the first time, we are moved by his empathy. His sadness is so big that he gorges on it. It was his absence of empathy, as the result of his addiction that cut him off from humanity. Now, ironically, it is through his insatiable despair that he is brought to hope.

This is not logical, and yet emotionally it makes perfect sense. We can't figure out our hero's transformation through a clear-cut formula. Rather, by inquiring into the structure questions, we are led to a more dynamic understanding of our story.

As we remain curious about what wants to be expressed through our story, we'll likely be surprised by where it takes us. We don't need to solve the riddle of our theme. We just remain curious and inquire, always moving from the general to the specific. As we continue to clarify what we're attempting to express, our story is revealed to us.

WRITING EXERCISES FOR TODAY:

As your hero, write for five minutes . . .

1. "My worst defeat was when . . ."

2. "I will finally rest when . . ."

Until tomorrow,
Al

DIAMOND DOGS
STORY STRUCTURE ANALYSIS

Let's take a look at the structure of *Diamond Dogs* based on the structure questions at the back of this book. (NOTE: Spoilers ahead. If you haven't read the book, you may want to do so before reading on.) Before we begin, remember that there are no absolute answers here. Our objective, through this analysis, is to develop a sense of the story's movement. By approaching structure in this way, we're less inclined to try to *get it right*, but instead to seek a dynamic relationship to our own story. For example, some writers think the end of Act One happens when Neil walks off the football field, while others think it is when he chooses to remain silent about the body missing from the trunk. The more important point is that our hero is always making choices and taking action. Ultimately, I don't really care which point is the end of the act (though I tend to think it's when he chooses to remain silent). In this way, we are not seeking a bull's-eye, but rather seeing how the plot points can happen in clusters, e.g., Neil might make a series of decisions that collectively propel him into Act Two. Story structure is not something to be answered or figured out; it is a paradigm that invites our story to be as dynamic as it wants to be.

WANTS AND NEEDS

- Neil wants to feel connected, so that he can move on from his past.
- Neil needs to accept the truth of his past, in order to feel connected.

Notice how the *want* is something outside of the protagonist, something he cannot control. The *need* is within, something that he is able to give to himself.

DIAMOND DOGS: ACT ONE

OPENING: How does my story begin? What is the initial experience? What images and ideas emerge?

• The story begins in the desert. Present day. This is a drama. Neil Garvin is frustrated, angry, lost and alone. His father abuses him. His mother is gone. Do we know what the story is about yet? Not yet. Do we have a sense of the world? I sure hope so.

DRAMATIC QUESTION: What is the dilemma in my story?

• Neil's dilemma is that he wants connection but he's afraid that if anyone knew who he was, they would not like him. He tells us, "I knew I had a secret. I didn't know what it was, but I knew it was terrible." This is the tension that carries the story to its conclusion.

INCITING INCIDENT: What event happens that sets my story into motion?

• Neil runs into Ian Curtis on the road, killing him. He puts the body in the trunk. Now we know what the story is about—secrets. Do you see the connection between this moment and the dramatic question of "How can I be connected to others when I have a secret?" This event provides a context for the theme.

OPPOSING ARGUMENT: How does my antagonist respond to the hero?

- Neil's father, Chester, is the sheriff. He discovers the body in the trunk, but remains silent. Remember, this is a story about secrets. Now we are beginning to see how every character in our story revolves around the dilemma. The dilemma is universal. Everyone wants connection, and everyone struggles with how much of themselves to reveal.

END OF ACT ONE: What decision does my hero make that he can't go back on?

- Chester gets rid of the body. Neil remains silent.

ACT TWO

FALSE VICTORY: What is the first sign of growth or success that my protagonist experiences toward achieving his goal?

- Neil has sex with Mary. He makes a connection. The only problem is that she is the sister of the boy that he killed.

MIDPOINT: What event happens that forces my protagonist to respond? (This event often involves temptation. He could go back to where he was or forge into the unknown and risk losing everything.)

- Neil quits the football team in defiance of his father. The secret is haunting him. He is linked to his father in a way that he has been trying to escape his whole life. Though he remains silent about the crime, he refuses to remain silent about being his true self. This is the first moment that he stands up to his father.

SUFFERING: What does it look like when my protagonist realizes that this is more difficult than he had imagined? How does he suffer?

- Neil confesses to his best friend, Reed, that he killed Ian. Reed is being badgered by the FBI for information on Neil, and is torn between his loyalty to his friend and his responsibility to the law and to the family of the dead boy.

SURRENDER: What would it look like if my hero realized that what he was pursuing was impossible to achieve?

- Chester arrests Reed for Neil's crime. Neil suddenly understands the depth to which his father will go to keep a secret. Neil recognizes that if this secret is buried, he will become his father. This fear terrifies him more than getting caught for the crime he committed. If he gets away with this crime, he will never be free.

ACT THREE

REALITY: What is the truth of my hero's reality that he is beginning to accept?

- In Vegas, Neil recognizes that Bernice's handwriting is identical to the birthday card he got from his 'mother' when he was five. He is beginning to understand the reality of what happened to his mother.

ACTION: What action does my hero take as a result of accepting the reality of his situation?

- Neil confronts his father about what happened in the

past. This leads to the fight between father and son in the desert.

CHOICE: What image or event do I imagine when I think of my hero's want and need colliding (or coming into battle with each other)?

- Neil forgives his father. He recognizes the truth that his father killed his mother in an attempt to save his life. Neil unloads the bullets from his father's gun, averting a possible suicide. They turn themselves in to the authorities.

Hero returns home: What is the final image in my story?

- Neil is released from prison. He stops outside the fence and raises a hand to his father, who plays basketball with the other inmates. They see each other, perhaps for the first time. Neil can go back to his life without secrets and with a coherent narrative for his past.

WEEK 4: THOUGHTS AND REMINDERS

- Our hero's goal doesn't change, though his approach to achieving it is always changing.

- The hero's dilemma is frequently subconscious and becomes conscious for him as the story progresses.

- The hero's goal is less important than the meaning he attaches to it. The stakes are life and death. The meaning may seem unclear at this point. That's okay. It will be revealed in time.

- The hero's want is something outside of himself, like validation, permission, love, or an answer of some kind. It is something over which he has little or no control. What our hero needs is within. What he is seeking outwardly, he discovers he must give to himself.

- The plot points are not carved in stone. We approach the structure questions as an opportunity to cull images for the story. Rather than worrying about where they fit, we can let ourselves get excited that we are filling our well with images and ideas.

- The dilemma is personal to our hero, but also broad enough to be universal to everyone.

- There is a difference between suffering and surrender. When we suffer, we tend to dig our heels in. We fight against what may be inevitable. We surrender when we recognize that we have no choice.

HOMEWORK FOR THE WEEK

We are continuing to imagine the world of our story and getting more specific with our outline. We continue to hold it loosely, to let the story be whatever it wants to be. Please feel free to start writing prose. We have one more week of imagining the world of our story before we begin writing our first drafts, but of course there are no rules.

DAY 23

"Without words, without writing and without books there would be no history, there could be no concept of humanity."   —HERMANN HESSE

OUR STORY IS ALIVE

Hi Writers,

When we talk about structure and character, driving narrative, wants and needs, dilemma, transformation, surrender, theme, dramatizing exposition, and on and on...we can start to feel overwhelmed. How the hell can I do all of these things and feel free to write my story? For God's sake, the whole reason I got into this racket is because I wanted to have some fun!

Hemingway talked about writing one true sentence. Anne Lamott speaks about writing the story bird by bird. We can't figure the whole thing out. Our story is bigger than we are. What really matters is that our story lives. We don't want to sacrifice the aliveness of our characters for a limiting idea of where our story ought to go. Story structure is not a formula; it's an invitation to allow our story to be as dynamic as it wants to be. It's a way of organizing our thoughts, conscious and subconscious, into a coherent narrative. As we continue to inquire and hold our story loosely, even after we've written our first draft, we move toward a clearer and more specific understanding of it.

This week we continue to amass images and inquire into the structure questions. We allow an outline to emerge. We don't judge our emerging story. Do we need to have the whole story figured out? God, no!

Why we write is more important than what we write. We are writing our story because it has its grip on us. We're curious. We're seeking to understand, to make sense of something. Let's let go of the result so that we can allow our story to take us where it wants to go. Let's give ourselves permission to explore areas we might otherwise have assumed would not work. Our story's structure can contain anything we imagine. Whatever comes to us either belongs in our story or is a stepping stone to what ultimately belongs. Let's continue to inquire and to trust that we are being led. With every word we are growing as writers.

WRITING EXERCISE FOR TODAY:

Write for ten minutes . . .

"The truth I'm resisting in my story is . . ."

Until tomorrow,
Al

DAY 24

"Writing is a dog's life, but the only life worth living."
—Gustave Flaubert

BACKSTORY

Hi Writers,

We can't have a story without conflict. Conflict arises as our hero encounters worthy antagonists. Worthy antagonists are born out of a richly imagined back story. When we imagine the world of our story, there can be a tendency to believe that what happened in the past is not worthy of deep inquiry because it isn't going to be in the story. Without a clear and specific relationship to previous events, our story tends to be general and lacks narrative drive.

Every story begins with "Why is this day unlike any other?" This is the Inciting Incident. A series of events have conspired to provide meaning to this particular moment. When an actor prepares a scene, he often considers his character's moment before. This moment before informs his current state. It is the same with the characters in our story. A specific relationship to our minor character's backstory brings detail and authenticity to our work, and with our major characters it reveals surprises and reversals of plot. Remember, character suggests plot, and our characters are born out of the events that have shaped them.

In *Diamond Dogs*, Neil Garvin kills Ian on the highway. This is the inciting incident. However, the story is not simply about

"Will he get away with this?" Without the backstory of his mother's disappearance the story could go in any number of directions. The backstory informs the story.

For those who have started writing prose, if you feel like your story is getting *chatty*, or that you are telling and not showing, be curious about the backstory. This may provide a clearer and more specific context for present events.

WRITING EXERCISES FOR TODAY:

As your hero, write for five minutes . . .

1. "My best memory is . . ."

2. "My worst memory is . . ."

Until tomorrow,
Al

DAY 25

"Trust only movement. Life happens at the level of events, not of words. Trust movement."
—Alfred Adler

MOVEMENT

Hi Writers,

We are going to write the first draft so fast that we don't have time to think. Right now we are doing the heavy lifting of imagining the world and inquiring into the structure questions. We are seeing our characters in relationship to each other and getting a sense of the movement in our story.

We are nearly ready to write our first draft. We have a sense of the beginning, middle and end, though there may be vast reaches that seem vague. That's okay. Our characters are alive. We have not silenced them by imposing some idea of what should happen upon them. All we have to do is listen to them and get out of the way. Even when it seems that they are taking our story hostage, we can give them a little rope. We must allow them to make choices, to surprise us. This leads to movement. Character is revealed through conflict. It is through a character's choices that our story turns.

Our characters are like little children at the mall who run off, terrifying their parents. Where are they going? Are they safe? Let's let them play! Let's allow them to terrify us a little bit. It is all going to work out. Writing is an act of faith, but not an act of blind faith. We have faith in structure. We have a basic framework for the journey. We can trust that within the framework we have imagined, our characters have some latitude to explore the vastness of their experience.

We may be concerned that our story doesn't 'fit' into the traditional structure paradigm. Structure is simply a way of organizing all of our ideas into a coherent narrative. It is a paradigm for transformation. There is no formula to this. We are interested in structure as a way of stretching our imaginations and making our story as dynamic as it wants to be.

Someone asked me if the hero could appear for the first time near the end of Act One. Why not? Plenty of historical epics tell the story of generations of a family and the hero may not even be born until deep into Act One. Again, there are no rules. We just have to ask ourselves, "Why am I making this choice?" As we explore the nature of what we're expressing, we begin to see how malleable our story is. A reader must be invested in the plights of our characters and curious about the outcome, otherwise he will simply stop turning the pages.

Continue to ask, "Why am I making this choice?" If an answer doesn't reveal itself to you, trust your gut. There is much we are not supposed to know until after we've written the first draft. The thing that stops so many writers from completing their work is the belief that they're supposed to know something before they've written it. If we knew it all, there would be no reason to write it.

We may only understand the movement in our story in retrospect. While I was writing *Diamond Dogs*, it seemed completely illogical to me that Neil would quit the football team right after he had killed the kid on the highway. Why would he want to draw attention to himself at this point? And yet that was what the character was insisting upon. Only later did I see the myriad repercussions of this choice on the story.

WRITING EXERCISES FOR TODAY:

As your hero, write for five minutes . . .

1. "When I look in the mirror, I see . . ."

2. "If you knew me before, you would have said . . ." Write from the point of view of the hero at the end of the story.

Now do these as an antagonist in your story.

Until tomorrow,
Al

DAY 26

"There's a lot of tasteful writing out there—nice, tidy, clean—but sometimes it's excess, rawness and the unpolished that work."   **—DAN VYLETA**

WITHHOLD JUDGMENT

Hi Writers,

When we give ourselves permission to write poorly, we start telling the truth. This process strips away convention. It may feel strange at first, perhaps even like a betrayal. That is just the voice of resistance. We can listen to it all we want, but we don't have to believe it. Resistance is out to stop us from telling our truth. There is only one way to battle resistance, and that is to write our story.

BE KIND TO THE ARTIST

If we are going to do the hard work of writing a novel in 90 days, it is important that we reward ourselves regularly. We are asking our subconscious to really swing the hammer, so let's give it a break each day. There are many great right-brain activities: hiking, rollerblading, walking, showering, driving, rocking back and forth in a prone position, yoga, refinishing furniture, painting . . . okay, you get the picture. These activities are wonderful for accessing the subconscious. The artist needs space to dream.

EVERY OPEN HEART HAS AN ANTAGONIST

As I write this, Gustavo Dudamel is beaming from the front page of the *L.A. Times*, clutching his heart and swooning to the heavens. Last week, a journalist urged us not to get too excited about L.A.'s newest conductor, counseling us that he was still young and unproven, that we should not rush to anoint him genius quite yet. The other day, President Obama won the Nobel Peace Prize and his critics cried that it was too soon, that he had not done anything yet.

Dudamel and Obama are not ignorant men. They are aware of the dangers of leading with their hearts. They are human and not impervious to criticism, yet they choose to proclaim themselves in spite of the blowback. What if Dudamel read last week's article and decided to be more emotionally careful, that the cost of public scrutiny was not worth his bruised ego? In a creative life, the fear of embarrassment threatens us at every turn. We feel the pull to lower our vision, to withdraw, to become practical and sensible, all those words that masquerade as maturity but are really just euphemisms for fear. As artists it is important that we do not underestimate the antagonistic forces we face in the act of creation. Our fears are not unfounded insofar as we have evidence to support them. And frankly, if we face them head on, the antagonistic forces will win. After all, they are armed with libraries of proof. The desire to transform means risking everything we think we know for something beyond our imagining.

By taking the risk of allowing ourselves to be used as a channel we become targets for every cynic and naysayer for miles around. We must protect our creation by not discussing it while it is being born. We cannot wait for everyone to support our endeavor. We cannot wait for everyone to approve of what we have to say. We cannot wait for the coast to be clear, for our security to be guaranteed, for victory to be certain. We alone know what the truth is in spite of the inner voices that may tell us otherwise. There is no time to settle a score. There is nothing to win. When we write from an open heart, we are aware of all the arguments and yet all of the reasons that our antagonists can muster can never prevent the light from coming through the cracks.

WRITING EXERCISES FOR TODAY:

As your hero, write for five minutes . . .

1. "My epitaph will probably read . . ."

2. "I would like my epitaph to read . . ."

Until tomorrow,
Al

DAY 27

"Example is not the main thing in influencing others, it's the only thing." —**ALBERT SCHWEITZER**

SHOW, DON'T TELL

Hi Writers,

Show, don't tell: the mantra of every screenwriting teacher. Film is a visual medium in which character is revealed through behavior. As novelists, we are afforded the luxury of exploring the internal lives of our characters, but this can sometimes be misunderstood by the novice fiction writer as "telling, not showing." He can sometimes become so absorbed in the internal lives of his characters that the story collapses into burdensome exposition. The writer doles out more and more backstory in a desperate attempt to get the reader caught up so the actual story can begin. The art of storytelling is in disguising or dramatizing information so that the reader is compelled to continue turning the page. The art of storytelling, regardless of the medium, is dependent upon showing rather than telling.

Showing is objective. It allows us to draw our own conclusions. Do we trust what we are told in our everyday lives? Hell no! So why should we trust some dude we've never met just because he filled a couple hundred pages with words? When we are left to draw our own conclusions, a trust develops between author and reader. Telling is subjective and engenders distrust because it often carries an agenda. The storyteller must be more interested in the truth of his story than in his idea of the result. If he does not explore the worlds of his protagonist and antagonists with equal integrity, the reader will smell a rat. Readers are not interested in opinion. Readers are only interested in what happened, who said what, and who did what to whom. Story is nothing more than a series of beats that lead to our hero's shift in perception. This is a broad canvas on which to create, but it is a canvas. There is a context for the novel, and when that context is disregarded, it becomes something else: essay, manifesto, diatribe, journaling, or worse, therapy.

Showing is visceral, immediate. It allows the reader an experience. Telling is playing God. Telling is dictating what one ought to believe about a given situation. Telling is describing to the reader a version of what happened as opposed to laying out the action and allowing the reader to draw his own conclusions. Telling lacks energy and immediacy.

It either works or it doesn't. We're accountable to no one. We may write a story that's entirely in the mind, an anti-narrative screed that defies all known laws of structure, and nobody will come to our door and tell us to quit it. But after we step back from it and the dust settles, we may discover that we have shown the world something new.

So, how do we show and not tell?

When we focus on our hero getting what he wants and drop the need to explain everything, we begin to discover creative and dramatic ways to show the reader what he needs to know in order to move the story forward. When we find ourselves telling, we can just stop and ask ourselves what our hero wants and what is standing in his way. By focusing on our hero's want and his immediate obstacles, we move out of our heads and into the immediate conflict of our scene.

WRITING EXERCISES FOR TODAY:

As your hero, write for five minutes . . .

1. "My attitude toward sex is . . ."

2. "My philosophy on life is . . ."

Until tomorrow,
Al

DAY 28

"Imagine the story that you would most want to read, and then shamelessly write it."

—J. D. SALINGER

THE FIRST DRAFT

Hi Writers,

Tomorrow we're going to start writing our first draft. Relax. We have done the work. We are ready. Like actors who have prepared for a role, we can now let it all go and let the story be told through us. Our only job now is to log hours on the page. There are no rules, but it might be a good idea to set a goal for ourselves.

How does 750 to a 1000 words a day grab you?

This is manageable. Three or four pages. If we were to write four pages for the next sixty-two days, we would have a 248-page first draft. Of course, the amount you choose to write is up to you. Some writers have completed their first drafts while averaging 500 words a day, while others have written 150,000-word first drafts. Let's give ourselves permission to write poorly so that we can create a space for our imaginations to soar. Our first draft is rough. It may not always even make sense. That's okay. We are writing quickly in order to stay ahead of those sensible voices that want to keep us in our place.

Our novel is our priority. If we find ourselves at 11 p.m. having procrastinated for the day, we write those pages at our bedside. It's amazing how quickly the pages can get written when we're tired. When we commit to this task, our subconscious surprises us with its willingness to bring the thunder.

Lastly, we don't talk about our story to anyone. I have witnessed far too many unnecessary writer's block situations resulting from discussing a project in its early stages. The pitfalls far outweigh the benefits. Our story is sacred. The connections are far too tender and nuanced for even our conscious selves to understand. I know we often get excited about our stories and want to tell the world, or we get scared and want someone to assure us of our story's merits. Either way, we're getting into the result. Contain the energy. I strongly suggest that we carry our stories with us like a delicious secret for the next 62 days.

Our only job is to get to the end. We've been asking the structure questions and amassing images, fragments of dialogue, ideas and various possibilities. Do we need to know exactly how our story goes? No, that would spoil the fun. When in doubt, we just keep marching on towards our next plot point.

Our work for the week is simple. We're writing from the beginning of the story to the inciting incident. Today let's think about all that happens leading up to that point.

HOW LONG SHOULD MY NOVEL BE?

Do we have a sense of how long our book wants to be? Every story has its own pace and rhythm. Is it an epic novel like *Crime and Punishment*? Is it a terse crime novel like Raymond Chandler's *The Big Sleep*? It might be helpful to have a sense of proportion as we set out to write our first draft. Have fun!

WRITING EXERCISES FOR TODAY:

Write for five minutes on each . . .

1. "My hero wants . . ."

2. "My hero needs . . ."

Until tomorrow,
Al

WEEK 5

WRITING THE FIRST DRAFT

This week we begin writing the first draft of our novel. We are going to spend the next three weeks writing Act One. This week we are going to write roughly a third of the way through our first act to the inciting incident. We need to turn off our internal editor. This is our time to let it rip. Everything we write either belongs in the story or will lead us towards what ultimately belongs in the story. We cannot make a mistake.

DAY 29

"The last thing one knows in constructing a work is what to put first."   **—BLAISE PASCAL**

NARRATIVE VOICE

Hi Writers,

Who is telling our story? Should it be written in the first person or third person? Both forms have their particular challenges and opportunities. If your story is vast, with many characters and sub-plots, it might work best with a third-person omniscient narrator, the voice that knows all. It can tell the reader what is going on in the minds of all the characters and follow all of the action simulta-neously. An omniscient narrator makes it easier to broadly depict the novel's events from a variety of viewpoints.

The third-person narrator is like a detached observer that sits on our hero's shoulder. Third-person narration tells the story from the hero's point of view or perhaps from the perspectives of a few different characters, but its scope is limited.

A story in which the reader learns information as the hero does might benefit from first-person narration. This story is told from the "I" perspective. We're taking the reader inside the mind of one character and seeing the world through his eyes. We can hear his unique point of view, his patois, which can be a lot of fun. *The Catcher In the Rye* and *To Kill a Mockingbird* are both excellent examples of strong, distinct first-person narration.

Again, there are no rules. It might be a story that uses first and third person. It could even be told in second person as Jay Mc-Inerny did in *Bright Lights, Big City*, e.g. "You walk into the room. You see him. You melt."

We have done the heavy lifting of imagining the world. We are ready to let the story be told through us.

THE FIRST DRAFT: THREE CARDINAL RULES

1. Just tell the story. Don't worry about the prose. Don't worry about grammar, syntax, spelling or research. That can all be addressed in the rewrite. Just get the story on the page.

2. Keep going. Some days are better than others. Don't stop writing because you hit a rough patch. Don't judge the writing. It's difficult to be objective about our writing when we're in the middle of it. Keep going and get to the end.

3. Don't rewrite. Do not go back and edit. Do not cross anything out. At this point, it is too early to know what will ultimately belong in the story.

Until tomorrow,
Al

WEEK 5: THOUGHTS AND REMINDERS

- If we feel hemmed in by an outline, then we can hold it as loosely as feels right for us.

- We give ourselves permission to write the forbidden.

- We will concern ourselves with grammar, punctuation and syntax in the rewrite.

- Don't be too concerned with logic. Trust your intuition. Allow yourself to be led to revelations that would not have arrived had you said, "My character would never do that."

- Our story is not going to look exactly like what we thought it would. That is not a bad thing.

- Show, don't tell. We dramatize exposition by putting our characters into conflict and keeping them there.

- We let the story find its own pace.

- If it feels like our story is flatlining, we inquire into our worthy antagonists. How are they standing in the way of our hero achieving his goal?

- We write as quickly as we can while paying attention to the beat-by-beat details of our story.

- We don't go back and rewrite anything. If there is a significant change (if our hero decides he is a doctor and not a sportscaster, fine, make him a doctor and keep going) we can go back and fiddle with it in the rewrite. When we go back, there can be a tendency to get stuck.

- Act One involves setting up the scenario that gets paid off in Act Three.

- Research can be another form of resistance. We probably need to do far less than we think. We care about human beings in relationship to each other, and if we're writing about furry creatures or aliens from another planet, they're still just a metaphor for the human struggle. We can always do more research after we have written our first draft.

- It is a challenge for every artist to get her work done in the midst of a busy life. If possible, early mornings are a good time to write. We are rested and have yet to confront the psychic barrage of the day. If we can get the writing out of the way first thing, the rest of the day may go more smoothly.

HOMEWORK FOR THE WEEK

1. Write a quick outline of the events leading to the Inciting Incident. Don't spend more than ten minutes on this.

2. Begin writing the first draft of your novel. This week we are writing to the inciting incident. Let's set a page count goal and stick with it. Is it 750-1000 words a day? At that rate, you will have 5250-7000 words by next week. We will spend three weeks on Act One.

Note: You are not writing to the end of Act One this week!

DAY 30

"All great works and all great thoughts have a ridiculous beginning. Great works are often born on a street corner or in a restaurant's revolving door."
— **ALBERT CAMUS**

THE END INFORMS THE BEGINNING

Hi Writers,

We're not writing our entire novel today. We don't have to solve every story problem today. All we have to do is show up and write our pages. Let's set a manageable goal and meet it. Let's make it a habit. We follow our characters to our daily specified goal and our work is done for the day. If we want to do more, that's great – but consistency is the key. Let's trust that as we do this day by day, our story is revealed. And let's drop the idea that it has to be flawless the first time through. Let's give ourselves permission to take risks, to get wild on the page. No one is going to read our first draft and following the rewrite, no one will be the wiser. Our only job is to let our story live.

As we begin, it's helpful to have a sense of our ending. We don't need to have it all worked out; we just need to know what we're writing toward. The protagonist in every story has an arc. Whether it is from ignorance to wisdom or from fear to love, it is invariably the journey from belief to knowing. In the beginning our hero has an idea of the way things are and in the end, he has gained a fundamental understanding of his circumstance. Let me explain with another love analogy.

BELIEF VERSUS KNOWING

Let's say our protagonist wants a woman to love him. He believes if he's a nice dude, he'll succeed in his goal. He does cartwheels, turning himself inside out in his attempt to win her favor, but she wants nothing to do with him. Finally, he stops trying, and lo and behold, she warms to him.

So what did he believe? Perhaps he had an idea of what it meant to be in a relationship and feared he was not worthy. Perhaps he pretended to be someone he wasn't in order to be loved, and only when he stopped pretending was she able to see him for who he was. As a result of the journey, our hero knows something he did not know at the beginning. Perhaps he knows that he's all right, not because she comes to him, but because he was willing to let her go. Story often involves the journey of reframing an old belief in a way that supports our hero in his new life.

A belief is an intellectualized relationship to an object. It's often an idea that has been passed down. It isn't necessarily wrong; it just may not be the whole story. Knowing goes deeper, to the nature of something. Knowing is flexible; it contains paradox. It transcends dogma. At the end of our story, our hero has an altered relationship to what he believed.

Beliefs can be threatened, but knowing can absorb any threat. Knowing is different than certainty. Certainty implies a lack of curiosity whereas knowing is infinitely curious, because it involves a deepening relationship to the nature of the thing. When one knows, one welcomes opposition as an opportunity to deepen his sense of knowing. To know is to resolve the old paradigm of winning and losing. There is no right answer or wrong answer. There is just a search for the truth.

Example: Jack falls in love. Swept away, he suddenly understands what all the Barry White songs were about. He feels misunderstood by his parents. Obviously they have no idea what real love is or they would let him borrow the car to take Jill, the object of his desire, to the dance. But they don't and Jill dumps Jack for Chad because Chad has his own car. The devastation is unspeakable. Jack is shocked by the depth of his despair, causing him to question love. He makes meaning out of his circumstance. Does love exist? Is it possible to truly know another person? Perhaps he decides that love does not exist and he sets out on a course with this belief. Or he decides that love does exist but that Jill is superficial. The meaning our hero makes regarding his situation influences the actions he takes. Perhaps he meets Judy and falls in love again, but this time he finds out whether or not he will be rejected because he rides the bus.

We each have within us a fundamental knowing. We are uniquely qualified to tell our story, and if we can remain curious about our hero's belief it will lead us to our hero's shift in perception. As we imagine our hero at the end of our story, let's be curious about what he knows to be true.

Our lives have a way of creeping into our fiction. Let's remember that we're not writing the facts of what happened, but rather the *nature* of what happened. When I wrote *Diamond Dogs*, on some level I was exploring the nature of my relationship with my own father. However, I never played high school football nor was my father a sheriff in Nevada. Those details were just a function of the world of my story. I wasn't attempting to recreate my life on the page in order to work something out. That is not the domain of fiction or even memoir. We cannot solve our lives in fiction and we must never confuse writing with therapy. Telling a story without a sense of why we are telling it can be a setup. The solution is to imagine our hero at the end of the story. What has he come to understand? How have his relationships altered as a result of his journey? This will connect us to the reason why we are telling the story in the first place.

Until tomorrow,
Al

DAY 31

"Technique alone is never enough. You have to have passion. Technique alone is just an embroidered potholder."   **—RAYMOND CHANDLER**

KEEP GOING

Hi Writers,

We don't need to force anything. We allow the truth to be told, even if it seems, at times, temporarily at odds with our idea of the story. Sometimes it may seem that we're off course, but as we stay with it, we discover a deeper truth. As our hero moves toward his goal, he encounters obstacles, and we might be surprised that he's not doing what we thought he would. This doesn't mean that we're doing it wrong.

At this point we're in no position to go back and edit. Our only job is to write to our projected goal for the week. The first draft is very personal. Sometimes I'll even write stuff I know won't make it to the second draft. I just need to get it out. Writing the first draft might even bring up big feelings. Terrific. We don't need to get hung up on them. Feelings are like Portland weather—they're going to change in a minute.

Also, it's helpful to be curious about what's going on in our own life, and to ask where the nature of this experience lives in our story. Once we're tuned into our story, the universe has an uncanny way of feeding us our lines.

• Get excited by the conflict.

- Explore the opposite direction of where you think the scene is heading.

- Allow yourself to be surprised.

Lastly, don't worry about overwriting. In the rewrite you will trim it down to what is essential.

Until tomorrow,
Al

DAY 32

"I think it's bad to talk about one's present work, for it spoils something at the root of the creative act. It discharges the tension."   —NORMAN MAILER

DRAMATIC TENSION

Hi Writers,

We're always struggling to be heard, to be approved of, to make rent, to pay our health insurance, to hold onto the love we've found, to negotiate household chores, to be respected for our brains and not our beauty, to appear caring when we don't give a shit, to appear indifferent when we care deeply, to find the answer that will relieve us of our struggle, and on and on. Investigate the tension in the scene. Be specific.

If we're feeling bored or confused, we can get quiet and explore the truth of our hero's struggle. The irony is, it will bring us relief and lighten our mood. Be willing to write the forbidden! There's a reason we're telling this story. There's something we want to say. As a matter of fact, it's so important we say it that the dread of not getting it right sometimes masquerades as boredom. But guess what? It's not our job to get it right! We're merely channels. Our job is to inquire. Let's leave the heavy lifting to our subconscious. Our job is to be kind to ourselves and to show up every day on the page. Aren't we more productive when our boss treats us well? As we inquire, our story tells us all we need to know in time.

WHAT IF MY ACT TWO FEELS VAGUE?

Sometimes we're clear on one part of our story, while other sections feel pretty vague. If Act Two still feels unformed, trust that you have a couple of weeks to clarify what's coming next. As our story reveals itself, we develop a more specific relationship to it. While we write our first act, we can continue to take notes on our story and allow an outline to emerge. Oftentimes the inspiration we need shows up just in time.

Until tomorrow,
Al

DAY 33

"I've always just wanted to earn my living by writing. The best thing is to go into my study in the morning and put words together." —ROBERT HARRIS

COMMITMENT

Hi Writers,

Writing the first draft of our novel is the most important thing we'll do over these 90 days. When we commit to this goal and create a regular time and place to explore on the page, the writing can feel almost effortless. But when we try to squeeze the pages in between a million other things, we experience resistance.

Sometimes we kid ourselves that this is sedentary work, that it does not engage our entire being. Writing our first draft is a marathon. We must pace ourselves. We must stay with it, take the hits when they come, and be grateful for those days when the story rushes at us so fast we can barely keep up.

I'm frequently asked by writers where I think an event belongs in their outline. It's not a question I can answer. The story lives fully and completely within you. We must let the event tell us where it belongs. We don't ever want to abdicate our story to some one else. It's important that we continually let go of the belief that someone else might know more about our story than we do.

However, an event in and of itself cannot be randomly deposited into the story. If we are unsure about where it belongs, we may perhaps want to step back and be curious about what we are trying to say through the event.

If we used a historical event, like the bombing of Pearl Harbor, we can see how that could be an inciting incident, a decision at the end of the first act, a moment of surrender, or the battle scene. The incident could happen virtually anywhere in the story. The event is irrelevant without context. We provide context by understanding what we are attempting to say through the event. For one writer, the bombing might be the end of the story, and for another writer, it could be the beginning. The meaning we assign to the event is in relation to our hero's goal.

Until tomorrow,
Al

DAY 34

"The writer, when he is also an artist, is someone who admits what others don't dare reveal."

—ELIA KAZAN

WE CANNOT MAKE A MISTAKE

Hi Writers,

Story is not something that can be intellectually deconstructed. It's too complicated, and yet the paradox is that when we inquire into our characters and allow our story to be revealed to us, it's impossible to make a mistake. Everything we write either belongs or is leading us to what ultimately belongs in the story. We've imagined a series of events that lead to our hero's transformation. Even if we don't understand why it's being written, we can trust that when we've completed our first draft we'll begin to see patterns that will lead us to a more specific understanding of our story.

Our job is to allow our story to lead us as it moves toward its inevitable outcome. What we think is a mistake is often an opportunity for a richer story. We may frequently feel stuck or that we've put our hero in a position that seems at odds with who we thought he was. The Roman philosopher Terrentius said, "Nothing human is alien to me." It's not our job to decide what our characters do, but rather to inquire into the choices they make. This leads us to a richer understanding of who they are. We begin to understand the endless paradox of human experience through these fictional people. Don't negate. Explore creative ways to support your character's choices. This is our opportunity to get it all down on the page as quickly as possible. In the rewrite we'll have an opportunity to explore why we wrote what we wrote, but for now, let's just get to the end.

Until tomorrow,
Al

DAY 35

*"The most common way people give up their power
is by thinking they don't have any."*
—ALICE WALKER

SELF-AUTHORITY

Hi Writers,

There can be a strong tendency, especially for new writers, to want validation as soon as possible. A friend of mine is a very successful Century City lawyer. In the seventies, he was not only a successful young litigator, but was also an up-and-coming novelist. He had published three novels in fairly quick succession to some acclaim and *TIME Magazine* had just named him one of the ten brightest new stars in fiction.

On an international flight he scribbled down twenty pages of what he had planned to be the beginning of his fourth novel. He got home, thrilled with what he had written, and showed it to his wife. Her response was lukewarm. Actually, I can't remember exactly what he told me her response was, because I was too stunned by his: he stopped writing.

The creative path is littered with the towering potential of unfinished manuscripts. We're all fragile and sensitive (in fact, it's our sensitivity that informs our creativity) and sometimes, in an attempt to steel ourselves against criticism, we objectify the act of creation. We distance ourselves from our story as if it that will protect us.

We measure our work against others and look outside of ourselves in the hope of avoiding future disappointment. This is simply another manifestation of the myriad ways in which our inner critic wants us to stay stuck. It tells us the lie that only a rare few are born artists. It's a good one, because it can prevent us from ever bothering to start. Our deepest fear is that we fools will be mocked by wasting our lives in pursuit of an endeavor that will reap little reward.

At some point the writer must stop measuring his passion and surrender to it. When we direct our focus to simply telling our story, the thrill of creation becomes its own reward.

Expecting too much too soon can be a fatal mistake. Of course we should strive for excellence, but excellence in the first draft involves dancing with the muse, not self-flagellation. We must develop a self-validating mechanism—and we must not show our work to others until we are ready. I don't think my friend ever decided to quit writing. Perhaps he began to doubt his story. Perhaps this doubt led to distraction, and then, finally, to creative paralysis. Quitting is rarely a conscious decision.

Sometimes I wonder if he will ever finish his fourth book. He probably won't. But I don't think that our creative spirit vanishes. It just transmutes. When we abdicate authority over our work we're prone to distractions and mischief. When we allow ourselves to be influenced by well-meaning reasonable folks, our subconscious dulls and we fall into lockstep with all of the other drones.

Inquiry is a defiant act. We cannot ask for permission. All of the logic and reason in the world means nothing in the face of truth.

Until tomorrow,
Al

WEEK 6

ACT ONE:
THE OPPOSING ARGUMENT

Our idea of the story is never the whole story. Even with an outline, we must be willing to hold our story loosely in order to allow it to go where it needs to go. This week we are writing roughly two thirds of the way through our first act. In Act One we are setting up the story by exploring the most dynamic ways to reveal the nature of the dramatic question.

DAY 36

> "A writer writes not because he is educated but be-
> cause he is driven by the need to communicate. Be-
> hind the need to communicate is the need to share.
> Behind the need to share is the need to be under-
> stood."   —LEO ROSTEN

I DON'T HAVE ENOUGH SCENES

Hi Writers,

A series of events need to happen to inform our hero's decision at
the end of Act One. The stakes are rising. What situations will lead
to the moment that our hero makes a decision?

We can't be afraid to put our protagonist in hot water. Writing involves putting our characters in jeopardy and then wondering how they can get out of it. We may notice that our protagonist
is experiencing an inner struggle.

The struggle might be between the desire to belong and the
desire to be true to oneself, or the desire to succeed might be at
war with the desire to take a shortcut. The struggle is universal,
something that everyone can relate to. Act One ends with our hero
making a decision that will lead into the rising conflict of Act Two.

Be curious about your hero in conflict with his antagonists.
What does he want? What is the argument against him achieving
this goal? How can you show this? Notice how these questions
might inform a more specific relationship to your antagonist.

In Act One of *Diamond Dogs*, when Neil comes home with the body in the trunk, we discover that his father is the local sheriff. Making Neil's father a lawman helps to explore the dilemma. As the author, did I do this consciously? Not quite. I was simply seeking to heighten the jeopardy, and in pursuit of this, my subconscious took care of the rest.

We have two more weeks to finish our first draft of Act One.

Until tomorrow,
Al

WEEK 6: THOUGHTS AND REMINDERS

- We cannot make a mistake. When a plane flies to its destination, it is off course 95% of the time. As our hero moves toward his goal, he is going to encounter obstacles. A good story contains disappointments, temporary triumphs, and reversals of fortune before our hero is returned home.

- If our writing feels stale, let's be curious about what we're trying to protect. What is the deep fear that we are unwilling to reveal? Let's be curious about our antagonist and willing to show the conflict. Remember, we love to the extent that we hate.

- What does our hero's unresolved state look like? Are we willing to write from that raw, vulnerable place?

- If we are not connected to the tension, we should stop writing, take a breath, and be curious about the specific conflict between our hero and antagonist. Put them into action. The stakes are life and death.

- Our subconscious performs miracles on demand. It is not our job to figure out how to get to the end. Our job is to have a "sense" of the ending. Is it a story of courage, love, hope, redemption, revenge, or is it a cautionary tale?

CHECKLIST OF QUESTIONS

1. What does our hero want? What are the choices she is making?

2. Are we meeting the main characters early on?

3. Is the conflict established early on?

4. Do we understand the dilemma at the heart of our story?

5. Is there tension?

6. Do we care about our hero?

7. Do we have a clear inciting incident?

8. If our story begins with a lot of explaining and back-story, let's be curious about the present urgency for our characters.

9. Where does our story turn? What surprises are in store for our characters? Remember, our story is not linear. It is building on itself. Just like life, one incident leads to the next until we are in a place we never expected to be.

10. We are not married to our outline. We are interested in the spirit of the outline, the driving want of our hero. The incidents and events may change.

HOMEWORK FOR THE WEEK

1. Flesh out your current outline with all of the moments, ideas, and images that lead up to the beginning of Act Two.

2. Find a middle point between your Inciting Incident and the end of Act One. Write to that point by next week.

DAY 37

"The cat sat on the mat is not a story. The cat sat on the other cat's mat is a story." —John le Carre

CHARACTERS BEHAVE UNCHARACTERISTICALLY

Hi Writers,

When there appears to be an intractable story problem, we don't have to solve it—we can get excited by the complication. The number-one rule of improvisation is "don't negate." Always say yes. We approach the first draft the way a child makes up a story. A child is endlessly inventive, telling her story with a spirit of playfulness, and when asked a question, she always has an answer.

Yes, this is serious business, but when we take ourselves too seriously we get bogged down in our idea of our story. Our characters can go anywhere and do anything! Our job is to find reasons to support their choices. This means that when we have an impulse, rather than negating, we must explore reasons that support the action. Let's face it, we probably each do about three far-fetched things every day! What is drama if not the examination of characters behaving uncharacteristically in response to unusual circumstances? Anything is possible: a murderer averts a crime, a nun robs a bank, a solid marriage falls apart overnight, the nerd gets the girl, the spinster falls in love, an angry man smiles, the shy girl breaks into song, the extrovert is struck dumb, a miser donates his worldly possessions, a fool discovers the cure, a sea creature makes the leap to dry land...and grows lungs.

Story is evolution.

Characters are always behaving uncharacteristically. Our job is to support the behavior of our characters under the circumstances our subconscious has dreamed up.

Until tomorrow,
Al

DAY 38

"If you're not making mistakes, then you're not doing anything. I'm positive that a doer makes mistakes."
—JOHN WOODEN

PERMISSION TO WRITE POORLY

Hi Writers,

The fear that we are doing this wrong is bound to arise, but it is often tied up with the idea that we're supposed to know how to do it. Our story is bigger than we are. We are merely a channel. Our job is to inquire. When we put our curiosity before our fears, we will get to the end.

We are writing our first draft quickly, but not rushing. We must allow the details to emerge. Some parts may feel like a sketch while others feel like an oil painting. This process is methodical, but each scene should feel as fully drawn as possible before moving on.

Writing a story is a process. It's revealed to us a little at a time. If we continue to inquire and stay out of the result, it will have a chance to live.

Until tomorrow,
Al

DAY 39

"The two most engaging powers of an author are to make new things familiar, and familiar things new."
—SAMUEL JOHNSON

STORY STRUCTURE

Hi Writers,

What do we want others to understand through our story? Does our hero learn to accept himself? Does he learn to love, to commit, or forgive? Does he lose what he most valued but finally reclaim something he thought he had lost forever? The *plot* is simply the outward means through which we explore an inward journey.

Our hero wants something. This desire is related to a deeply held belief that getting this thing will, in some way, change his life. As we track our hero's want through the plot points, a throughline reveals itself. In the first draft, though we have a sense of the journey, we are still flying by the seat of our pants. This is as it should be. We need to allow our subconscious the latitude to surprise us – otherwise we will merely be writing our idea of the story.

Structure is an immutable paradigm for transformation. It can contain the nature of anything we can imagine. The challenge is in marrying the wildness of our imaginations to the rigor of story structure.

In the 1950's, the abstract expressionist movement emerged in New York City. The movement attempted to capture an emotional or visceral experience on the canvas. In Mark Rothko's early work we can see evidence of his more mature work, but it is still busy and uncertain, as if he's trying too hard. Only after years of work did he arrive at the simple but stirring color-field paintings that secured his reputation. It is the same for writers. We struggle to reflect life through our perceptions while keeping our work anchored to our source, that place in us that knows all. Through this process we are reminded that we are not in charge. In the best paintings of the abstract expressionists, there is a sense of completeness for the viewer, a sort of "Yes, of course," moment that transcends our logical centers.

We are not attempting to simply recreate the facts of our life on paper or even *work out* our lives in fiction, but rather we are using these images and ideas as a springboard to take us into an experience. On one level, we are seeking to become lost in our story. This is why the structure questions are so vital. They are not a rulebook, but a guide into the underlying meanings in our work. They are the breadcrumbs that will lead us out of the forest.

Until tomorrow,
Al

DAY 40

"Against the assault of laughter, nothing can stand."
—MARK TWAIN

HUMOR

Hi Writers,

Humor connects us. It makes us care. It's a vital aspect of any story, adding depth, richness and humanity. Shakespeare understood that in order for the audience members to experience the impact of loss and betrayal, they needed breathing room.

Humor is about writing truthfully. In the midst of two characters attempting to get what they want, there is humor. There is humor in the absurdity of our misplaced priorities. There is humor in our desire to be good, to do it right, in our fear of being left out, our embarrassing need for connection, our awkward wish to be acknowledged, our petty desires for retribution. There is humor in our rage at not getting the parking space, and in our permitting great sins to be done to us for fear of appearing uncivilized. There is humor in our fragility. Humor keeps drama in check.

When a writer is accused of melodrama, it is not that the characters are overreacting, it is that the writer is. When drama becomes an excuse to indicate the largeness of our feelings or to settle a score, it loses its universal quality and our writing becomes journaling or therapy.

It is through levity that we break our readers' hearts. Even in the grimmest situations, with ruthless objectivity a writer can wring humanity from the moment.

As seriously as we take our work, finding humor in it only offers a fuller glimpse of the world.

Until tomorrow,
Al

DAY 41

"You don't write because you want to say something,
you write because you've got something to say."
—F. SCOTT FITZGERALD

OUR HERO MAKES A DECISION

Hi Writers,

We have nine more days to get to the end of Act One. At the end of Act One, our hero makes a decision toward achieving his goal. A moment of reluctance may precede this decision that propels him into the new world of Act Two. He will encounter all sorts of unexpected obstacles for the first time. He will have to grow and adapt. Should he remain in stasis or take the risk? His reluctance to change builds tension. Our conception of what our hero's decision should be may alter as we continue to plumb the depths of the tension at the heart of our story.

As we move into the middle of our first act, we are probably learning new information about our characters that may inform our hero's decision. It is helpful to be curious about the specific circumstances surrounding his decision, as they can provide us with the necessary material to set up this moment.

Until tomorrow,
Al

DAY 42

"It belongs to the imperfection of everything human that man can only attain his desire by passing through its opposite." —SOREN KIERKEGAARD

OPPOSING ARGUMENT

Hi Writers,

It is easy to get lost in our idea of the plot, but that will not get us to the end. Our focus ought to lie squarely with our protagonist's attempts to achieve her goal. It is from this place that our plot emerges.

Here are some questions to ask ourselves:

- Do we have a basic confidence in the order of events that lead to the end of the act?

- Does the tension build through our first act?

- Are we showing and not telling?

- What are we discovering about our characters as we witness them in conflict?

- How do these new character revelations inform our story?

- What is the decision our hero makes that she can't go back on?

- What are the obstacles she encounters that lead to
  the inevitability of this decision?

As we approach the moment at the end of Act One in which our hero makes a decision, the key is to be as specific as possible. The reason for the decision is connected to our hero getting what she wants. And what she wants is connected to an idea of what it will give her, e.g., "I want love because then I will feel worthy." It's not necessary to intellectualize the want, but simply to have a sense of it. The want is the catalyst that motivates him to move forward.

WRITER'S BLOCK

Writer's block is simply an absence of information. There is something we need to understand in order to continue. We just aren't sure what it is. This is where the structure questions and stream-of-consciousness exercises come in handy. As we continue moving forward with our first draft, keep a separate pad of paper to scribble down thoughts and ideas as they emerge. If we allow ourselves an objective distance from the story we'll be led to an answer. It may not be the answer we'd expected. It might be much better.

Remember that we have a basic sense of what our hero wants and the journey she takes. Let's trust that and allow our story to take us wherever it wants to go.

Until tomorrow,
Al

WEEK 7

ACT ONE:
OUR HERO MAKES A DECISION

O ur goal for this week is to reach the end of Act One, the moment when our hero will take action toward achieving his goal. Be curious about the reluctance around this decision. Our hero's reluctance connects us to the dilemma.

DAY 43

"I guarantee you that no modern story scheme, even plotlessness, will give a reader genuine satisfaction, unless one of those old-fashioned plots is smuggled in somewhere."   **—KURT VONNEGUT, JR.**

PLOT

Hi Writers,

We might be convinced that a certain scene must happen, but as we begin writing it we discover the scene does not want to be written as we'd imagined it, and perhaps even not at all. We must trust this. We must follow the scene where it wants to go. Underneath our idea of what happens, our subconscious is searching for the most effective way to explore a satisfying resolution. It's important that we continue to hold our plot loosely in order to stay connected to these underlying forces.

Our story accumulates meaning as it progresses—it's about something. The plot is less important than the story's underlying meaning. When we allow our characters to surprise us, the plot is often realized in a fuller and more surprising way.

I used to worry about the infinite number of ways I could get the story wrong. I felt like I was walking a tightrope and that with one bad choice my story would collapse. We can become lost in our fixed idea of the way it should all go. Yet haven't we all had the experience of losing a piece of writing and in rewriting it we discover how much of it we had actually retained? Our story was not residing in our brain. It sprang from a deeper place. We were not required to remember it. What we want to express is embedded in our DNA. We need merely to relax and be curious, to hold it loosely, and allow our story to be revealed to us.

Until tomorrow,
Al

WEEK 7: THOUGHTS AND REMINDERS

- We are not doing this alone. It may sound strange, but when we commit to a creative endeavor, we tune into a channel and all sorts of coincidences may happen that support us in completing our work. Trust them. The universe is helping us.

- In order to complete our work, we may experience a shift in priorities. Sometimes our friends and family don't take kindly to this. This does not mean we are bad or selfish. It just means that the garbage will get taken out tomorrow.

- We may also notice that we have become a filter for our story and our daily lives. The people we hear and see, our environment, everything, informs our work, giving us insights and ideas.

- "I'm not writing, but I'm thinking." Some days we don't put as many words down on the page. That's okay. Sometimes writing is pondering.

- Let's be curious about the metaphors in our story. Metaphors illuminate the story's deeper meaning. Our story is bigger than the plot. If all that happens is what happens, our reader will be dissatisfied. We are curious about the nature of what we are expressing. This makes our story universal.

- If a scene or an idea comes to you, write it down. If your characters seem to be taking on a life of their own, be curious about how you can support their choices.

- Be curious about a moment of reluctance that precedes your hero's decision at the end of Act One. Humans don't typically like change. We only change when we have run out of choices.

CHECKLIST OF QUESTIONS:

1. Have I introduced the major players in my story?

2. Do I understand their relationships to each other as functions of the story?

3. What is my hero's dilemma?

4. Do I have worthy antagonists?

5. Is the story moving through action? Am I showing rather than telling?

6. Do I have a sense of the decision my hero makes at the end of the Act One?

7. Am I being specific?

8. Do I feel engaged with the tension or am I just logging words on the page?

9. What is my story about? Do I feel on track with this? Do I have a sense that I am exploring the story in a compelling way?

HOMEWORK FOR THE WEEK:

Write to the end of Act One. This is where our hero makes a decision that he can't go back on.

DAY 44

"Writing is its own reward."

—HENRY MILLER

IS MY STORY GOING TO WORK?

Hi Writers,

Story often begins with a character or a premise that ignites our imagination. We want to know more, to see how it will play out. With rising anticipation, we follow every new revelation. However, at some point it's inevitable that we want to take the wheel. We become so invested, this work so important, that we feel we must figure it out ourselves. Nothing engenders panic more quickly than thinking we should know something we don't. It's an archetypal dream: A man walks past Carnegie Hall to see on the marquee that he's conducting a Mozart concerto that night. Except that he's not a conductor and has never heard of Mozart. Panic ensues.

When we let go of the idea that our story is a problem to be solved, we can relax. Ideas and images naturally emerge.

There can be a period of time when the story doesn't seem to cohere. We may be compelled by a series of disparate images, or a sense of our hero at different points in the story, and wonder how on earth he is going to get from here to there. This can make us nervous, or it can thrill us. As long as we continue returning to that initial impulse, our story has a way of telling us where it wants to go.

Our subconscious is forever searching to find order in chaos. We have a built-in evolutionary drive. Our subconscious mind is the ultimate Mr. Fix-It. We don't ever need to crack the whip. In fact, it's when we crack the whip, through anxiety and fear, fretting about whether the writing is any good, that our subconscious starts shutting down.

It seems that the more we show up for our writing, the less credence we are inclined to give our anxiety. Every day is different and there is little connection between our feelings and the quality of our work. Writing becomes a practice, something we do each day without question or expectations. We surrender to our curiosity, and our story reveals itself to us in ways we may never have imagined.

WHAT IF I'VE FALLEN BEHIND?

Perhaps you haven't written in the past few days. Don't beat yourself up. We all struggle with resistance, but unless we quit, resistance can't win. Get back on the horse. See if you can write to the end of the first act by next week. If not, give yourself an extra week. Make a contract with yourself that you will finish your first draft by Day 90 . . . and you will. Will it be perfect? Of course not! It's not supposed to be. Use the first draft for its intended purpose—to get the basic story on the page.

Until tomorrow,
Al

DAY 45

"Books choose their authors; the act of creation is not entirely a rational and conscious one."

—**SALMAN RUSHDIE**

WE ARE UNIQUELY QUALIFIED TO TELL OUR STORY

Hi Writers,

Look at what we've accomplished in a month and a half! We have imagined the world, outlined our story, and are nearing the end of Act One.

Congratulations!

Remember that this is our first draft. As we continue to move from the general to the specific, there will likely be passages and entire chapters that feel unclear. We just write through them as best we can and continue to follow the story wherever it wants to take us. It is not possible to dance with our muse while second-guessing our footing. We move forward with excitement, allowing the conflict to mount as the story builds on what has happened previously. And if we realize that an event needs to have happened in order to inform the next scene, we write as if it did, and we keep moving forward. We don't ever want to hinder the drama simply because we haven't set something up. We can set it up later in the rewrite.

This is a right-brain process. Let's get excited by the wonderful surprises that arrive just in time rather than worrying about what has not yet been revealed. There are things we can't know until we get to the end. We can spend years obsessing on a chapter or we can write the first draft quickly, and in doing so we may discover the inspiration that eluded us by simply getting to the end.

If we are surprising ourselves our readers will be surprised.

Until tomorrow,
Al

DAY 46

*"Trust the instinct to the end, though you can render
no reason."*   —RALPH WALDO EMERSON

UGHH . . . WHAT AM I DOING?

Hi Writers,

I told my wife that I didn't know what to write today. She suggested
I talk about my own experience.

Frankly, yesterday was a sumbitch.

I put in my hours. I got through a few scenes, but the truth
is, I was restless, distracted, grumpy, and fearful. I questioned every word. I won a couple of small battles, but it felt like a slog.

What I do know is this: I've been here before and it didn't
kill me. I know that I can't control the quality. I know that I can't de-
pend on my feelings to be an honest gauge of the work. I know that
it is difficult to remain objective when I'm down in the middle of it.
I also know that I do have a story to tell, that when I imagined the
world and allowed a rough outline to emerge, there were moments
that excited me. The characters intrigued me and a few interesting
turning points were revealed. And most of all, I had a sense of the
ending and it felt satisfying, like there was a real journey for my
protagonist. That helps me relax a little. I have something. I may not
completely understand it, but I know it holds a lot for me.

Does my story work? That is always the question I want to
ask, but I'm not sure that it's the right question. When I am in the
middle of it I don't believe that it's possible to be objective. I have

to trust that I have something valid to say. From that, the story will emerge. I do know that if I surrender the outcome and remain faithful to the process, the mist will clear and I will begin to see what I've got. I know that if I put my curiosity before the result I stand a chance at creating something of value.

Yesterday I had to dig deep just to stay with the process. I had to remind myself of what I tell everyone else, "Be willing to write poorly." I must give myself this permission, not because I want my writing to suck, but because I can't control the quality, and putting pressure on myself to make it good will kill any chance of that.

Yesterday there were no wondrous passages. I don't believe that my prose soared or that I caught lightning in a bottle, but I made some progress and moved a few pages closer to the end.

Today is a new day.

Until tomorrow,
Al

DAY 47

"A blank piece of paper is God's way of telling us how hard it is to be God."   —SIDNEY SHELDON

BACKSTORY . . . REVISITED

Hi Writers,

As we write, backstory questions arise that beg to be answered in order to move our story forward. This is inevitable. We can't fully imagine our backstory before we write. The exciting thing about this process is that we have made a contract with our subconscious to finish the first draft in 90 days, which puts it in turbo-charge mode. We are marching toward the end and there is a sense of urgency (but not panic) that these questions must be answered at once. Sometimes we just need to go for a walk around the block and carry the question with us. If we can hold it all loosely, we may discover that our story is morphing into something other than what we had imagined, yet paradoxically closer to what we set out to express.

If our story wants to go somewhere, we can let it go there. We have an outline, a sense of the journey, but within that framework we must allow our imagination to soar. It doesn't even have to make sense. We may only understand its significance in retrospect, and if it leads to a dead end, we can delete it in the rewrite.

It's liberating to know that we *don't know* our whole story. When a seemingly mad idea pops up, we must follow it in our minds for a moment to see where it wants to take us. In the first draft, we cannot assume that we know with total precision the direction our story is heading. By exploring the opposite direction, we may discover it is a temporary detour that offers a more fully realized conclusion.

Until tomorrow,
Al

DAY 48

*"A king, realizing his incompetence, can either del-
egate or abdicate his duties. A father can do neither.
If only sons could see the paradox, they would understand the dilemma."* **—MARLENE DIETRICH**

MORE ON THE DILEMMA

Hi Writers,

Before we began writing our first drafts, we imagined the world
of our story, and held all of the ideas loosely. Although there were
some apparent contradictions, we had a very basic sense of a beginning, middle and end. As we write our first draft we begin to make
more specific choices. Where we had imagined the scenario in
broad terms we are now writing it moment by moment. Our choices become more defined. But how are these choices made? Are they
random? Though it may appear so, I don't believe there is anything
random about this process.

All of our characters revolve around the dilemma at the
heart of our story. Our characters are all functions of that dilemma.
The dilemma anchors our story. It is what we continually return to
and ruminate on, whether consciously or not.

The dilemma in our story is universal in that it is something with which we all struggle on some level. We don't have to
be a Southern father to understand the nature of Atticus Finch's
world in *To Kill a Mockingbird*. The story explores the dilemma of

remaining true to one's ideals in the face of opposing forces.

The challenge is to trust that what may feel random is being written for a reason. We may not understand it right now, but our subconscious has the ability to make connections that our conscious mind does not understand. As we write each day, our trust in our subconscious deepens. A certain knowing develops.

Until tomorrow,
Al

DAY 49

"If you want to do everything until you're sure it's right, you'll probably never do much of anything."
—WIN BORDEN

THE RELUCTANT HERO

Hi Writers,

No one likes change. The unknown is scary. The end of Act One involves our hero making a decision she can't go back on. There is often reluctance that precedes this decision as she weighs her options. Even if the reluctance lasts but a moment, it's an important beat in any story. Be curious about this reluctance as it will further develop tension. For example: A character might decide to reveal a secret to another character (an irreversible decision). But just because she wants to share her secret doesn't mean that there's no reluctance in sharing it. What if the other character betrays her, judges her, or rejects her? The tension between "What if I do?" and "What if I don't?" will add nuance to the moment.

Our hero is always making decisions, but the end of Act One has a special flavor. This decision will irrevocably change things. The hero is leaving the familiar for the unfamiliar. This decision could look like anything from a first date to sleeping with someone to accepting the promotion or moving to Bora Bora. It's not so much the action taken, but rather the meaning attached to this decision. The reluctance helps the reader understand specifically what our hero is struggling with. By inquiring into the reluctance, we may discover a moment that makes our end of Act One more dynamic and specific.

Although we are not all writing traditional narratives, there is still real value to inquiring into this question of a decision. Regardless of our story, the structure questions will invariably lead us to a more specific and dynamic experience for our characters.

A STATE OF DISCOVERY

Each day that we write we discover our own process. We begin to understand that there is no right way to create and that our objective is simply to allow the story to live. The first draft is a near constant state of discovery. Some revelations may seem counter to the direction we thought our story was heading in. We may even discover surprising things about ourselves. We discover that we're not always nice, that we're opinionated, that we have a dark side, or that we're bothered by things we think should not bother us. We may discover that our tolerance for bullshit has gone way down. We may discover that our perception of the world is widening while our certainty on any particular topic is starting to relax.

Perhaps we are noticing practical details, like a preference for writing in the morning or on buses that circle the city at 3 a.m. We may discover that after a few hours we are done for the day. Some writers write for six hours a day while others put in an hour. There are no rules. Our process is our own and each is valid.

As long as we continue writing and make it a habit, it doesn't matter how it gets done. The most important thing is that we stick with the process and remain curious. Our work is simply a paper trail documenting our journey back to our truest selves.

THE INTERNET: PROCEED WITH CAUTION

Sometimes the deeper we get into our story, the more we seek distraction. The Internet will suck the life out of any writer. It will turn the most disciplined among us into bug-eyed addicts. Not only can it swallow great chunks of our precious writing time, it can also assault the senses and steer us away from the stillness of our source. I urge any writer to avoid it until the writing is done for the day. The same goes for phone calls, grocery shopping, and going to the gym. Writing requires more concerted focus than any of these other tasks.

Until tomorrow,
Al

WEEK 8

ACT TWO:
OUR HERO EXPERIENCES FALSE HOPE

Following our hero's decision, he enters a new realm. This week we are going to write to the moment that our hero experiences initial success toward achieving his goal. As we do this, we are giving ourselves permission to surprise ourselves . . . and to write poorly. Giving ourselves permission to write poorly does not lead to poor writing, but its opposite.

DAY 50

"The artist is not a person endowed with free will who seeks his own ends, but one who allows art to realize its supreme purpose through him."

—CARL JUNG

STRUCTURE

Hi Writers,

Today let's look at a couple of things that may hopefully open us up to our Second Act. When we speak of structure, we are not speaking specifically about plot. Character suggests plot. Plot is the external vehicle through which we are able to track the internal shifts of our hero that lead to his transformation. Another way to think of it is like text on a computer. Underneath the text is coding, a system that allows us to understand the text. Story structure is the social coding that allows us to track our characters' actions. This social coding has developed over millions of years of evolution and is as much a part of our makeup as our genetic coding. Just as our genetic code is unique to each of us, its structure is universal. We are programmed to seek belonging, to crave connection. We rarely question these primal impulses. They are our nature.

Characters constantly make seemingly illogical choices that our readers will not question provided we support these choices with sufficient context. In *Diamond Dogs,* Neil puts the body in the trunk not because he is heartless, but because he fears his father's response.

BLIND SPOTS

As we track our story, we often find areas that feel unexplored. It's normal to have blind spots. I think of a blind spot as an idea of something that is not the whole truth.

The desire to write is the desire to evolve. We are seeking to understand something that we don't yet fully comprehend. In working with the structure questions, which address key points in our hero's journey, we've had an opportunity to explore these blind spots. In doing so, our perspective widens. Nobody wants to be in denial. It's a survival strategy. As we begin to understand the nature of our situation it becomes preferable to live in reality because it is only from this place that we can effect real change.

Blind spots can be used as opportunities for our story to become more dynamic by provoking us to question our preconceptions. Why did I decide that my hero was happily married? Is this an assumption based on my idea of the story or is this, in fact, the strongest choice for my story? What if he is just pretending to be happily married? What if he is actually carrying on a double life? What if . . . ? What if . . . ? Something may come of this inquiry. If not, we will have a clearer sense of why we must stick with our original idea.

In *The Adventures of Tom Sawyer*, Tom doesn't want to whitewash the fence. What does he do? Does he bribe a kid to do it for him? No. When the neighborhood kids tease him for having to work, he explains that this work is a joy. The kids beg him to let them paint the fence. Finally, he relents and deigns to let them labor. Imagine that you are the author for a moment; to have Tom refuse to let the other children paint the fence is counter to his desire. Oftentimes we arrive at what we're trying to express by inquiring into our preconceptions.

The paradigm of winning and losing is often shattered in

story because ultimately, there is no such thing. There is only cause and effect, action and consequence. Let's be curious about the assumptions we've made about our characters and open to exploring new directions. This may lead to blind alleys or it might open up our story to some stronger choices. Either way, we have nothing to lose.

Until tomorrow,
Al

WEEK 8: THOUGHTS AND REMINDERS

- We should have completed Act One today. If you have not, you may want to give yourself a day or two to summarize what happens so that you can keep moving forward. Of course, there are no rules. Everyone's process is different.

- If you find yourself going back and rewriting, you may be setting yourself up to get blocked later on.

- The hero's decision is connected to his goal. This desire keeps us on track with our story. It keeps us connected to the underlying meaning of what we're trying to express.

- We are going to spend four weeks on Act Two.

- This week we are writing to the point where our hero achieves a success of some sort, which may reveal itself to be a short-lived victory. *easy . find map → home →*

- When our hero achieves success, there is an identifiable shift for our hero. *feels hope ?   encounter C.B.*

- We can't resolve a story at the same level of consciousness that created the premise. This means that we must always be willing to explore the opposite choice. If we believe our hero idolizes her mother, how might our story be altered if she also despised her? Is it possible that both experiences are true? What situations might suggest this apparent contradiction?

- We want our reader to experience our characters' emotions through action and incident, not by telling them what they are feeling.

HOMEWORK FOR THE WEEK

This week we begin writing Act Two. Write to the moment that your hero achieves an initial success. Is there a moment where your hero recognizes the possibility of getting what she wants? What does that look like?

DAY 51

*"I have no special talent. I am only passionately
curious."*   **—ALBERT EINSTEIN**

ASKING THE RIGHT QUESTIONS

Hi Writers,

In *A Portrait of the Artist as a Young Man*, James Joyce states that his job is to "forge in the smithy of my soul the uncreated conscience of my race." He is saying that he is a pioneer. Writing requires courage as we are forever pressing up against our doubt.

As storytellers we attempt to create something that is bigger than ourselves. The problem arises the moment our brain registers the potential for failure. It wants to protect our ego from a fatal blow. When our limiting ideas clash with our dreams, we become overwhelmed and wonder, "Why is this so difficult?" And our trusty brain provides us with answers. It reminds us of our lousy childhood and our inferior education, or perhaps the tragedy of our privileged upbringing and idyllic experience at a leafy liberal arts college that robbed us of our fire. Perhaps we worry that our birth order indicates we are not the creative one, and on and on. Of course when we do this our subconscious shuts down.

The process of getting the story from our imagination to the page involves asking the right questions. When we turn our attention to the story and let go of our anxiety, the story comes to life. It's not that tough once we get the hang of it. Like any habit, it takes practice, and then it's just about maintenance.

Our conscious mind is like the CEO while our subconscious is the rest of the company, toiling away in the recesses. The CEO doesn't know how everything works. He just gives the orders, but if he's good, he asks lots of questions because he understands that the drones are running the show.

Until tomorrow,
Al

DAY 52

> *"Don't be afraid of appearing angry, small-minded, obtuse, mean, immoral, amoral, calculating, or anything else. Take no care for your dignity."*
>
> **—MARY KARR**

ASKING "WHY?"

Hi Writers,

Our subconscious is perfectly designed for this process. It already knows the story. Our only job is to remain curious. As we do this, our story comes into focus. It takes patience. When we get scared, we must inquire into the nature of our fear. When we get cocky, we must inquire into the nature of that as well.

When I investigate the nature of the dilemma at the heart of my story, I'm investigating the universal. Whether conscious or not, our desire to write is a desire to explore the nature of something larger through a particular event.

In essence, we are asking, "Why?" I tortured teachers with this question. "Watt, quit asking why!" "But why?" "Because . . . that's why!"

There is something primal about this question. Children ask it incessantly. Asking why is essential to getting underneath the events in our story. A fundamental truth is underlying these events. Our ideas are not necessarily wrong, it's just that they are not the whole story. It's brave work to challenge one's beliefs, but artists are brave. Through our story we seek revelation, that moment when our perception widens and we're liberated from some idea that kept us tethered. For a long time the idea may have provided a sense of security, but somewhere within us lies the desire for a greater freedom.

Until tomorrow,
Al

DAY 53

"Here's the secret to finishing that first book. Don't rewrite as you go."   **—ALLISON GILMAN**

LAYERING INFORMATION

Hi Writers,

If you are looking at your outline and wondering how you're going to get all that you've imagined into your novel in 90 days . . . relax.

Story is a dialogue between our self and our ideal reader. As a story unravels, a bond develops between the reader and the author. Our reader is always asking questions and as we remain still and inquire, we instinctively respond to them. We become sensitive to the rhythms, the pacing, the amount of information required to keep our story moving forward. We don't need to show our reader every blessed blade of grass for him to understand that this is a lawn. Each moment we imagine does not require its own chapter. We can layer information into a scene.

Let's say our hero is a partner in a New York law firm and is about to lose his practice as the result of malfeasance. He is married with two kids, has a lover that lives downtown, and he has been selling arms to Pakistan in his spare time, which has been cutting into face time with his kids.

Do we need six chapters to convey all this information? No. Do we need a chapter to establish his character before moving the story forward? Of course not! Character is revealed through conflict. We could show our guy late at night working at the computer with the Empire State Building glowing behind him. He is sending the specs for the newest missile to his man in the Middle East when the phone rings. "Darling, I told you never to call me here," he says. His wife could enter his office and ask who he was talking to. He could tell her it was his law partner, and she could say that she thinks their daughter is coming down with her little brother's measles.

The more thoroughly we imagine the world of our story, the richer the story becomes. In the rewrite we will discover all sorts of creative ways to tighten our work and layer information to enrich the story with tension and detail while not running the length of *War and Peace*.

Lastly, don't worry about overwriting in the first draft. It can be tightened in the rewrite.

Until tomorrow,
Al

DAY 54

"Reverse every natural instinct and do the opposite
of what you are inclined to do, and you will probably
come very close to having a perfect golf swing."
—BEN HOGAN

MAKING THE SCENE DYNAMIC

Hi Writers,

If we have a sense of where a scene is going to end, let's explore its opposite. If I know a scene will end miserably for my hero, let me allow him an opportunity for hope. Isn't that how life is? We never know what will happen.

A constant tension lies at the heart of any dilemma. That tension is forever in play. It influences every word we speak, every thought we have, every action we take. We never want to indicate the ending of our scene. Within the scene is a struggle that precedes the outcome. Be curious about the specifics of the scene.

We don't know how events will unfold in our own lives, so why would a character know how a moment is going to play out in his world? Allow yourself to explore a variety of options before committing to a scene's end. This can open a window to aspects of our characters that we may not have otherwise considered.

Until tomorrow,
Al

DAY 55

"Action is eloquence."

—WILLIAM SHAKESPEARE

SHOW AND TELL

Hi Writers,

If we find ourselves telling what is happening in our story, it's okay. However, we probably don't want to stay on this track for too long. We want to get back to the action. We want to show what is happening even if that takes the form of an internal dialogue.

There is a difference between showing and telling. Telling is the author sticking his nose in things. It can feel like the author has a bone to pick. It reeks of agenda and engenders distrust in the reader. Showing allows the reader to make up his mind. The author vanishes and the reader becomes lost in the story.

In the opening of *The Catcher in the Rye*, Holden tells us about "all this madman stuff that happened last summer." He tells us that we're likely going "to want to know all about his lousy childhood and all that David Copperfield crap," then tells us he can't get into it because his folks are "very touchy" and "would have about two heart attacks apiece" if he talked about it.

Is Salinger telling or showing? Well, he is showing. Sure, the narrator is giving us information, but in fact we are experiencing this character as he tells us everything by not telling us anything.

Ha Jin's novel *Waiting* begins with the sentence, "Every

summer Lin Kong returned to Goose Village to divorce his wife, Shuyu." We are being given information that transcends the factual by containing a whole world of possibilities and thus igniting our curiosity. Our reader will have an emotional connection to our work through showing, not telling. If I tell you that the quest for the American Dream can lead to nightmarish results, you likely feel nothing. But when you read *The Great Gatsby* or *The Day of the Locust*, the reality of that statement comes to life.

Telling the reader what the characters are feeling does not mean that the reader will have the same experience. No one wants to be told what to feel. If we are being specific and building the tension, the reader will likely be invested in the story.

In the rewrite we will concern ourselves with editing, shaping, and the refining of prose. Right now, we are just telling the story, getting it down on the page quickly, before we have time to think.

Until tomorrow,
Al

DAY 56

"All truth passes through three stages. First, it is ridiculed. Second, it is violently opposed. Third, it is accepted as being self-evident."

—ARTHUR SCHOPENHAUER

BE WILLING TO WRITE THE FORBIDDEN

Hi Writers,

Remember when the earth was flat and homosexuality was a mental illness and rock 'n' roll was going to destroy the fabric of our society? At one time these ideas were actually taken seriously. People clung fiercely to them, convinced that to loosen their grip would mean catastrophe.

Sometimes we do this with our story. We can be so certain about the way it ought to go that we are unwilling to entertain other more dynamic possibilities. As we move toward the midpoint in our story the stakes begin to rise. We have a worthy antagonist who is standing in the way of our hero getting what he wants. At times our idea of the conflict feels flat, yet we're not sure how to raise the stakes. We may even sense an aspect of our characters that we resist fully exploring as it might feel like we're opening a can of worms. What if we lose control of our story, or it takes us in a direction that feels like a betrayal of someone we love?

What if we allowed ourselves to write the forbidden, even if it seemed at odds with the direction we thought our story was going? Isn't Schopenhauer talking about the ah-ha moment, when something suddenly becomes self-evident?

Story reveals a transformation. Is it possible that our resistance holds the keys to this shift in perception? We must drop our ideas of good and bad, right and wrong, winning and losing. Story is about cause and effect, action and consequence. We cannot stack the deck against our antagonist. We cannot begin our story by indicating the ending. Our hero does not become free by being good. Freedom is earned by shedding an old belief. This is why we are uniquely qualified to tell our story, because through our story we are inquiring into a belief that wants to be shed. We can only do this by exploring our character's shadows.

Let's explore the shadows with some quick stream-of-consciousness questions.

1. What is our hero's sin?

2. Where is our antagonist's joy and compassion?

3. What is our hero's regret?

4. Where is our antagonist's vulnerability?

5. When is our hero cruel, disorganized, small-minded, selfish, weak-willed, petty, controlling, manipulative, or ignorant?

6. When is our antagonist kind, supportive, thoughtful, funny, or selfless?

If our hero rides a white horse and our antagonists wear pointy moustaches, no reader will relate to our story. We are interested in the truth of this world. Without exploring the shadows, we will be lost in our idea of the story.

The irony is that the more we are willing to trust the truth of our characters, the more powerful our hero's transformation will be. What if we allowed ourselves to at least inquire and explore each impulse that comes to us, even if it feels a little dangerous? What if we gave ourselves permission to write this story for our-

selves? What if we gave ourselves permission to withhold all judgments until the end? What if we entertained the possibility that we
did not need to even understand where our story was taking us?

As I write this, do you hear your hero shouting, "But you
don't understand!"? Is it possible that our hero's transformation is
on the other side of this violent opposition? Is it possible that we
are on the brink of something, that we are pressing our noses up
against what is about to be revealed as self-evident?

Until tomorrow,
Al

- portal is the false hope
- commit is destroying
└ knowing he
was to
destroy
it

WEEK 9

temptation is to

THE MIDPOINT: *go back*
OUR HERO COMMITS
knowing the danger?

OR

At the midpoint of the story, our hero realizes that there is no going back. This is often where the story *turns*. As we continue to investigate our hero's motivation we may discover a moment of temptation for him. This moment will keep us in touch with the tension at the heart of his dilemma.

is it the glimpse
of a new kind of
happiness?

DAY 57

"Show me a writer with third act problems, and I'll show you a writer who can't make a commitment."
—CLIFFORD ODETS

THE MIDPOINT: COMMITMENT

Hi Writers,

In the coming week, we are writing toward the midpoint of our story, when an event precipitates a response from our hero. This event is an outward illustration of our hero's dilemma, which may have been kept under wraps.

In Alice Sebold's novel *The Lovely Bones*, Susie Salmon's father Jack suspects that his neighbor George Harvey raped and killed his daughter. He goes to the police demanding that they arrest George, but they refuse. It appears that George is going to remain free and continue living across the street from Jack's family. This raises the question of how Jack and his family can return to their lives without closure.

The midpoint often involves the hero becoming conscious of his dilemma. It is not imperative to articulate the dilemma, but rather to be aware that the tension in the story is directly related to it.

It is only as the result of an event, e.g., the police refusing Jack Salmon's request that they arrest George Harvey, that our hero commits himself with greater investment toward achieving his goal. This often involves pursuing a new approach, e.g., Jack takes matters into his own hands. It's only when our hero is aware of the consequences that there can be a moment of great temptation.

This is often a major turning point in the story. The stakes are heightened as a result of our hero understanding the nature of his situation and making a choice based on this new understanding.

The stakes are always raised through complication. For example: A couple falls in love and gets married. They both want to have the best marriage possible, but each partner has a different idea of what that should look like. He might think it means working hard at his career and providing for the family. She might think that it means working hard at her career to provide for the family. But who's taking care of the family? She might agree to put her career on hold for a few years to raise Junior, only to grow resentful.

But then the story turns.

Remember, our hero's goal doesn't change, but her relationship to what she wants is always changing. The midpoint might be where she commits to a career at home. Perhaps she invents an environmentally friendly diaper and begins selling it on the Internet. Business takes off. Working from home, she takes care of Junior while managing a staff. Problem solved, right? No. Because the problem was not about our hero being a stay-at-home mom.

Let's say the guy is jealous of his wife's success, but he can't say anything because she is the one who made the compromise. The dilemma at the heart of the story might be "How can I live my dreams when they don't look like what I thought they would?" The midpoint could be where she commits to a career at home. It's a reversal. The story turns. Ultimately, the couple will understand something about themselves, and the result will lead to a new equilibrium. Either their marriage will grow stronger or it will disintegrate.

Until tomorrow,
Al

WEEK 9: THOUGHTS AND REMINDERS

- Midpoint: An event happens that causes our hero to respond by committing fully toward getting what she wants.

- Be curious about: 1) The want (what is driving our hero), and 2) The dilemma. These two elements are linked. As we explore the want and the dilemma at this point, we may be led to a specific image for our story.

- Commitment is different than simply making a decision at the end of Act One. The stakes are raised. Our hero understands the consequences of her choice, namely that there is no going back, thus leading to a moment of temptation.

- At the midpoint, be curious about how your hero is responding to the worthy antagonists.

- If you haven't reached the first plot point of Act Two, set a goal for yourself to complete it in the next day or two. Feel free to sketch it in and move on.

- Don't worry if the story doesn't completely make sense.

- Don't feel like you must save some exciting plot point or revelation. Don't feel like you must vamp until the next great moment. Cut to the chase. Be curious about the possibility that if you play your ace, the story will not collapse, but it might go in another direction that you had not anticipated.

- Keep going. Don't look back. Don't dig up the seed to see how the story is growing.

HOMEWORK FOR THE WEEK

1. Write a quick point-form outline up to the midpoint.

2. We are writing to the midpoint, the moment where our hero commits fully to getting what she wants.

DAY 58

"Where there is no antagonist, you cannot quarrel."
—JAPANESE PROVERB

WORTHY ANTAGONISTS

Hi Writers,

If our story does not have worthy antagonists, there will be little movement for our hero; our story won't turn. There will be no surrender, no transformation. We must inquire into the nature of our antagonists. Let's be curious about why our antagonists behave the way they do. What do they desire, and how do they prevent our hero from achieving his goal? It's not our job to determine which characters are *good* and which are *bad*. Story is about action and consequence in service of a larger meaning. At its core, our story is an investigation into some primal aspect of humanity. Is it about respect, ambition, power, vanity, justice, equality, honor, jealousy, shame, freedom? Let's remember that our antagonists and our hero both want the same thing, though they go about it in different ways.

As the stakes increase, we may also find that we are confronting all sorts of fears. This is inevitable. When fears arise, it's important to stay connected to our hero transformed. Our fears can be convincing, especially if we make meaning out of them. But if we investigate the nature of our fears and are curious about where they live in the world of our story, we can make them our ally. Our fears are a way into our story, not a way out of our story.

If we're writing a memoir, there can often be a fear of hurting a loved one. This is understandable. It's why we must give ourselves permission to write the story for ourselves first, without concerning ourselves with what we'll do when the project is completed. If we don't give ourselves permission, there can be a tendency to try to control the story. The fact is, though the truth can sometimes be painful, it isn't cruel. Cruelty is remaining stuck to our old idea. It is only through inquiry that we are able to reframe it. We must write through our struggle, exploring the experiences of guilt, fear, anger, shame, in order to understand the real truth that is on the other side.

This is why it is important to set aside our moral judgments about our characters in order to explore why they are behaving in such a way. Notice how our hero and antagonists desire the same thing whether it is love, security, wealth, or acclaim. Their approach may differ greatly, but the desire is the same. Through the conflict between our hero and worthy antagonists we are attempting to make meaning of seemingly incomprehensible events in order to better understand our common humanity.

Until tomorrow,
Al

DAY 59

*"For strange effects and extraordinary combinations
we must go to life itself, which is always far more
daring than any effort of the imagination."*
—ARTHUR CONAN DOYLE

WRITING IS NEVER A WASTE OF TIME

Hi Writers,

Let's make no mistake—this mission we've signed up for is hard work. It requires patience and it helps to be gentle with ourselves. Sometimes we can get down on ourselves by thinking it should be easier and if it isn't we must be doing something wrong.

If we've ever done improvisation, we know the number one rule is to never negate. In improvisation, our task is simply to find a way to support what our partner has given us in order to advance the scene. This is exactly what we are doing. If we suddenly realize that our character is left-handed, we are curious about all that this means. If we suddenly discover that our hero was a golf pro in her earlier years, we're curious about how this experience has impacted her life, her relationships, and her new profession as the night guard at a toy factory. Every choice we make in our story has a ripple effect on the rest of the story. We must be curious about these effects. We can't control the world of our story. Our characters will resent us and our imagination will pick up its ball and go home. We need simply to trust that our subconscious is guiding us.

It will make the connections naturally. Our job is to remain curious about where we are being led.

We must stay out of the result and allow the story to be what it wants to be. Even if it feels like we are getting nowhere, we must trust that we are being led. There are good days and bad days. There are days when much of what we write may not make it to the final draft, yet these words were necessary to make room for the ones that will.

Until tomorrow,
Al

DAY 60

"The art of writing is the art of discovering what you believe."
　　　　　　　　—GUSTAVE FLAUBERT

STEPPING INTO THE UNKNOWN

Hi Writers,

Sometimes we come to a place in our story where we become careful. We are confronted with problems that seem unsolvable. I find it helpful to know that I don't know. I am truly confident that I am thoroughly incapable of figuring out the story in my head. This takes me off the hook and I can invite in the muse. Now, of course, this is not enough. This is where story technique comes in. I'm talking about the structure questions.

Artists are sensitive creatures, and without technique our sensitivity can consume us. We must use our sensitive natures to our advantage by asking the right questions. The structure questions remove our personal attachment to the outcome and we naturally become curious about the dilemma.

At the midpoint, let's allow ourselves to shuffle the deck so that a possibility emerges that may seem, at least initially, at odds with the direction in which we thought our story was heading. At the midpoint our hero steps off a cliff into the unknown. It can be thrilling or terrifying.

A reversal happens at the midpoint. It is often the result of the hero responding to an event. What does it look like when he is forced to proclaim himself? This may be where he is beginning to glimpse that what he faces is not merely a problem, but a dilemma. He is beginning to understand that with this commitment it will no longer be possible to go back to the way things were.

Step off the cliff and take the risk that you are being led.

Until tomorrow,
Al

DAY 61

"I assess the power of a will by how much resistance, pain, torture it endures and knows how to turn to its advantage."   —FRIEDRICH NIETZSCHE

RESISTANCE

Hi Writers,

If you find yourself battling distraction, procrastination, perfectionism, irritability, mild heatstroke, involuntary drowsiness, or anything else that tells you not to write today . . . you are not alone.

For me this week was tougher than most to stay focused. Teaching workshops, prepping an upcoming workshop, script due at end of month while rewriting a spec script and new novel concurrently. Family obligations, training a new assistant and three interns, getting regular exercise, blah, blah, blah. . . .

My solution. Get the writing done first.

And in the middle of it all . . . my old friend self-doubt. Yesterday I was a genius. Today I'm Ed Wood. I've been working on this project too long (my brain tells me) and I have lost objectivity. The one thing that keeps me going is knowing that my only job is to build a body of work. When I step back, I believe I am telling a story that is valid and true if I can just stay out of the way. I know this doubt will pass. I know that soon I will ship this puppy off and begin working on something else. My head tells me that the writing should feel more fun, and that I have run out of inspiration, that this racket is not for regular folk like myself.

In short, another day at the office. But I do know that nothing will prevent me from finishing. I detach from the highs and lows and remain focused on the task at hand. I continue to inquire and am grateful when I'm rewarded with new insight. I will eat and rest and tomorrow morning I will tackle the beast again.

Until tomorrow,
Al

Scissors kick

DAY 62

"In fashioning a work of art we are by no means free, we do not choose how we shall make it but . . . it preexists us and therefore we are obliged, since it is both necessary and hidden, to do what we should have to do if it were a law of nature—that is to say, to discover it."   **—MARCEL PROUST**

THE ROAD TO FREEDOM

Hi Writers,

Am I really going to top Proust? That pretty much says it all. All I can add is that there actually is a process to all of this. It's mysterious at times, maddening and ephemeral, but it's also simple.

I need simply to show up, to hold my space, and to inquire. In doing this, great things can happen. We begin to glimpse the realm that lies beneath our story, beneath what we may have initially thought our story was about. We are developing a relationship to the throughline.

As I inquire into the nature of my story, I may begin to see the glare of my own reflection. Where does this story live in my own life? What challenges am I being invited to confront?

Story asks everything of us for a reason. If it didn't, we would never surrender. The desire to write is the desire to resolve something we seek to understand. We can use our own life, our own experiences to explore the nature of what our characters are facing.

When we accept that it is human nature to have *fixed ideas*, and accept that what we believe to be true is not necessarily the whole story, we tend to relax and become open to new ways of perceiving our story's central dilemma. The paradox is that in accepting that we don't know the whole story, we move toward a resolution.

Until tomorrow,
Al

DAY 63

"Creativity requires taking what Einstein called 'a leap into the unknown.' This can mean putting your beliefs, reputation and resources on the line as you suffer the slings and arrows of ridicule."
—FRANK X. BARRON

MORE ON THE MIDPOINT / TEMPTATION

Hi Writers,

If you haven't reached the midpoint yet, don't fret. By the end of today, if you are not there yet, ask yourself if you're comfortable summarizing what happens up to the midpoint. If you're not, that is fine. There are no rules. Everyone's process is different. Just keep going.

If your story is feeling sluggish, you may want to consider writing a quick summary so that you can focus on the next step. Any sections that feel incomplete or not fully realized can be returned to in the rewrite. Let's keep moving the story forward. Remember, our goal is simple: Get to the end.

This next week is about writing from the midpoint to the point in the story where our hero suffers. The stakes are getting higher now. At the midpoint our hero may be tempted, but he steps off into the unknown toward getting what he wants. It is only after our hero takes the leap that he begins to understand the potential consequences.

It is crucial that we really listen to our hero at this point. If he wants to go in a direction that seems like it will collapse the story, we remain curious and open minded. We trust our hero's instinct. We allow our hero to say and do what he wants. By burning through all of our ideas of what we think our story is, we are able to reach a greater understanding. I know this may seem scary, as if our story might be prematurely resolved, but in fact, we are going to discover the opposite. We are going to discover the depth of our hero's commitment to getting what he wants. Our hero doesn't want the short-term fix. He wants the big Kahuna whether his ego likes it or not.

The desire we have created in our hero will be impossible to satisfy. The action he takes in Act Two will reveal the intractable divide between what he wants and what he needs. It is only by allowing our hero to take this step and move forward that he is able to discover the impossibility of getting what he wants.

Temptation is the word to remember at the midpoint. Be curious about how your hero is tempted, as it is this temptation that allows your reader to understand specifically what he's struggling with. If he isn't tempted, we may not understand the gravity of his desire. His temptation connects us to the throughline of our story.

Until tomorrow,
Al

WEEK 10

ACT TWO:
OUR HERO SUFFERS

The moment of suffering is a vital aspect of our hero's journey. Without it, there would be no context for a surrender. This week our hero questions the possibility of achieving her goal and she begins to suffer.

DAY 64

*"Man can learn nothing except by moving from the
known to the unknown."*   —CLAUDE BERNARD

STORY ISN'T LINEAR

Hi Writers,

Story isn't simply about a hero pursuing his goal and then succeed-
ing. Nobody would care. We're interested in our hero's shift in perception. We're interested in the journey that leads to his growth.
We're interested in what he comes to understand as a result of his
journey, in how he relates differently to other characters at the end
of the story. Our hero's goal never changes. However, his approach
to achieving it shifts constantly.

  If the theme of our story is *Love*, an argument is "Love conquers all." In order to explore an argument, we must be aware of
the opposing argument. For example, if we were to write about love
conquering all, we would explore all the ways that the desire for
love can lead to heartache. In fact, there will likely be a point in the
story in which our hero experiences grave doubts, even wonders if
love is a cruel hoax. The stakes rise as our hero pursues his *idea* of
love. His desire for love never changes. However, his approach (and
consequently the meaning he attributes to getting it) is constantly
changing. He might begin as a romantic, become a cynic, revive his
hope, and then find himself heartbroken before perhaps reframing
his relationship to love and understanding that in his pursuit, he

lost sight of himself. But his desire never changed from the beginning to the end. No one ever stops wanting love.

Story forces us to wake up. At times we think we have it all figured out and suddenly everything changes. We want to know the rules so we know what to do and where to stand. If only someone would give us the damn rulebook! But there isn't one, because if there were one, we would never wake up. As we learn the perceived rules, the rules seem to change. And this is what happens to the hero in our story.

This week we are writing to the point at which our hero suffers. He is beginning to understand how difficult his situation is. What occurs next in our story is a direct result of what happened previously. Sounds obvious, right? But it isn't! Here's why: Our idea of our story cannot be sustained for a few hundred pages. Our idea is actually quite limited. Consider this: If our story were a chess game, it would be akin to guessing multiple moves ahead. It isn't possible. We cannot guess where these characters are going to take us. Although we do have a basic sense of the journey from our outline, we must hold this loosely in order to allow our characters a certain freedom. As we inquire into the nature of our hero's desire, the next action will emerge.

Until tomorrow,
Al

WEEK 10: THOUGHTS AND REMINDERS

- Our story isn't linear. The trajectory shifts as a result of our hero's attempts to achieve his goal.

- The hero's goal doesn't change. However, his approach to this goal is always changing.

- Our hero suffers as he begins to recognize the difficulty of ever getting what he wants. He is awakening to the nature of the dilemma.

- Suffering is different than surrendering. When we suffer, we tend to dig our heels in, to put blinders on, and we limit ourselves to new possibilities.

- Surrender: the next major beat in our hero's journey happens as the result of letting go of the "want." Our hero still desires the same goal; it's just that he recognizes that his desire is preventing him from attaining it.

- If this moment feels unclear, be curious about your worthy antagonists. Every time our hero attempts to get what he wants, antagonists stand in the way.

HOMEWORK FOR THE WEEK

1. Write a quick point-form outline up to the moment our hero suffers.

2. Write to the moment the hero suffers.

DAY 65

"We were promised sufferings. They were part of the program. We were even told, 'Blessed are they that mourn.'"
—C.S. LEWIS

WHEREIN WE ALLOW OUR HERO TO SUFFER

Hi Writers,

No mother wants her child to suffer. And yet if she does not allow her child to experience distress, the child will never learn. It will be debilitating in the long run.

We are the mother to our protagonist.

If there is to be a transformation, we must be willing to put him in true jeopardy. We must allow him to suffer.

God allows Job to suffer in order to show the devil the depth of Job's devotion. Job's devotion to God transcends all of his worldly riches, including all of his ideas of what provides his life with meaning. Job's true nature resides in his spirit.

If we don't explore the depths to which our hero suffers, we will not understand why he surrenders. Our hero suffers as he begins to question why he ever set out on this journey. The vultures are circling and he begins to see that his options are limited. When a rat is cornered, it lashes out. When our hero suffers, his character is challenged and he may be forced to make a difficult choice.

Each moment in our story informs the next one. By making a connection between why our hero suffers and what he desires, we begin to see the dilemma. Our hero surrenders only when he has exhausted all other options.

Our hero suffers as a result of doggedly pursuing his goal. Suffering is an integral aspect of the hero's journey. It is natural to want to resolve conflict. As writers, we must be willing to sit in the space in which we may not see a way out, but remain curious as our hero moves headlong toward attempting to achieve his goal.

Until tomorrow,
Al

DAY 66

"A writer is a person for whom writing is more difficult than it is for other people."

—THOMAS MANN

FROM THE GENERAL TO THE SPECIFIC

Hi Writers,

In writing the first draft, we can have a revelation that thrills us while also causing us to reexamine what we thought our story was about. This can lead to self-doubt and fear. "Oh my God, I just wasted all this time writing something that isn't working."

While in the middle of writing our first draft, it's next to impossible to objectively read our own work. It's a given that a fraction of what we write will survive the rewrite process.

This is not bad news. It's the nature of the process. We're always moving from the general to the specific. Nothing we write is wasted. If we revere each word in our first draft as sacred text, we'll never get to the end. We sometimes need to burn through our ideas of what we thought our story was about in order to understand it in an intrinsic way.

We must not allow our latest revelation to become fodder for self-flagellation. Otherwise, we transform insight into an opportunity for panic and we begin trying to control the process. Instead, we should get excited that our work is becoming more specific. We must celebrate these revelations, and be curious about how our work can support the new revelation.

While rewriting *Diamond Dogs*, I consulted an FBI agent who explained to me that a sheriff would never allow high school kids to search for a body because they were untrained and would likely destroy any evidence. I panicked, fearing that a key moment in my story didn't work and would have to be removed; that my novel was built on a house of cards. I wondered if it was all about to come crashing down, and then suddenly I realized that the sheriff didn't want anyone to find evidence. What if he did it on purpose? Wow! Suddenly this terrible mistake I'd made became an opportunity to explore the nature of the sheriff in an interesting way. The tension shot up, the conflict with the FBI character became richer, and I probably only wrote a few new paragraphs to support this revelation.

The key is to relax and remember that we have something valid to express. When we stay connected to that ineffable impulse, everything falls into place.

Until tomorrow,
Al

DAY 67

"The foundation of all mental illness is the avoidance of legitimate suffering."   —CARL JUNG

MORE ON SUFFERING

Hi Writers,

Our hero is suffering. He had no idea it was going to be this difficult. Perhaps he is even wondering why he got started on this journey. And sometimes, as our hero suffers, so do we.

We are being led to a new awareness. Everything we need to know lives within. There is nothing to figure out. There is only something to leave behind. Perhaps it's a belief or an idea that our hero has about himself or the world around him. Be curious about what your hero wants, and the meaning he has made of it.

Our hero begins the story with a false belief. Dorothy believes that life will be better somewhere over the rainbow. George Bailey believes that he must leave Bedford Falls to have a wonderful life. Lin Kong in Ha Jin's novel *Waiting* believes that his life will begin when he finally divorces his wife, Shuyu. As these characters begin to suffer, notice how their suffering is directly related to the meaning they made out of their desires. It is not that their goals were invalid, but that the meaning they imbued them with robbed them of the present moment.

Our hero's willingness to suffer is a necessary beat that leads him to accept the reality of his situation. He is being led somewhere. Without exploring the depths of despair, there can be no surrender, no softening of the heart. One must experience death in order to be reborn.

Until tomorrow,
Al

DAY 68

"One of the symptoms of an approaching nervous breakdown is the belief that one's work is terribly important." —**BERTRAND RUSSELL**

MORE ON DESIRE

Hi Writers,

We all want things. Sometimes I think we are nothing but a collection of wants. Our hero's desire is not something to be intellectualized. It can be challenging to articulate at times, because what we want is visceral and can even seem contradictory.

When we remember people from our past, we tend to remember them through an emotional lens. Some people are joyful by nature, while others are melancholy, frantic or distant. It's the same with our protagonist's want; to intellectualize it would reduce the aliveness of the desire.

We want all sorts of things: love, belonging, adventure, security, purpose, meaning, respect, success, connection, revenge, loyalty, and so on.

Have you ever noticed that people exude the essence of their desires? In other words, whether we are conscious of it or not, we can actually sense people's desires. They are energetic, palpable. We can sense someone's ambition or envy or integrity or desire for closeness.

Sometimes what we want may seem contradictory. I want

to belong, but I also want to stand out from the crowd. I want to rebel, but also be approved of. These dualities are universal, and a well-told story reflects the vast contradictions of our characters' situations.

It is often through the contradictions that we are led to a deeper truth. At the end of *Jesus' Son*, the hitchhiking drug addict weeps for all the people he has never met or known. He is broken hearted by his first real glimpse of suffering. He has discovered sadness and through it he is finally able to connect to the world.

What we want unites all of our contradictions. Wanting to feel alive, for instance, can look like skydiving and it can look like working in a soup kitchen. Wanting love can look like marriage and it can look like divorce. It does not look like anything in particular, though we may initially believe it does in our story. What our hero wants is often something we discover in retrospect, something that becomes clarified as a result of having written our first draft.

Our hero's want never changes. We never stop wanting love or connection or meaning, though our relationship to these desires is always shifting. It is through the shifting relationship to our hero's desire that the dilemma is fully explored.

Until tomorrow,
Al

DAY 69

"Growth demands a temporary surrender of security."   **—GAIL SHEEHY**

Hi Writers,

TEN THOUGHTS FOR THE DAY

1. I have a worthy antagonist who will do anything to get what he wants. He is standing in the way of my ruthlessly onrushing protagonist.

2. I am completely open to where my hero wants to go and I am willing to be surprised.

3. When I am scared by this process, I will inquire into the nature of my fear. I will remain curious in the midst of my fear and I will stay out of the result.

4. I give myself permission to write poorly.

5. The first draft is simply about getting words on a page. I am allowing my characters to go wherever they want to go, and I have faith in the basic framework that I imagined in the outline.

6. My feelings are not facts. I understand that I am enormously invested in my story. I accept that I am going to be stirred up and I am willing to allow the images to pass through me as I continue to carry the torch.

7. Amidst my fear, I can still see that part of me that is willing to really expose myself on the page.

8. All I have to do is write 750-1000 words today.

9. It is okay if I don't know my ending today.

10. My subconscious is the seat of my genius. As I write this story, I am connected to this source. I can access it at any time. I am never alone.

Until tomorrow,
Al

DAY 70

"If you know exactly what you are going to do, what is the point of doing it?"   **—PABLO PICASSO**

COURAGE

Hi Writers,

It takes courage to suffer. When we have a sense of why we are telling our story, we are likely more inclined to explore our protagonist's suffering. We understand the necessity of this moment in moving our hero toward her transformation.

For a long time, I wrestled with trying to do it my way. It was only after I had had what I call a third act experience that I began to glimpse the mystery that the story is being told through me and I must surrender my idea of the story for the real story.

As writers, we are attempting to tell a story that somehow reveals more than we thought we knew. Logically, this is impossible, but when we allow our imaginations to soar without having to "figure out" a resolution, all sorts of new possibilities emerge.

The end of Act Two is often the moment when our hero lets go of his idea of what he thinks he wants. This idea is surrendered because he understands its impossibility under his current circumstances. I think of this surrender as a coin with two sides. On one side is despair and on the other side is a wider perspective. We surrender because we have no choice. We are hopeless, and recognize the impossibility of ever getting what we want. We let go of the pain of our desire, which does not mean that we give up our wanting, but rather that we reframe it. We assign it a different meaning. Thus it becomes possible for us to get what we want if what we want belongs in our life.

The creative act demands that we be a tiny bit more courageous today than we were yesterday. As we move toward the end of Act Two, we invoke courage to allow some of our hero's armor to fall away so that he can accept the reality of his situation.

We must ask ourselves, 'What is creating our hero's suffering?' It is precisely this suffering that will carry him to his surrender.

Until tomorrow,
Al

WEEK 11

END OF ACT TWO: OUR HERO SURRENDERS

Our hero surrenders because he has no choice. It is in surrendering that our hero reframes his relationship to his goal. Notice how all of our characters have a specific relationship to the goal (whether the goal is love, wealth, social standing, etc.) and that often what separates our hero from an antagonist is a willingness to surrender and reframe his goal in order to get what he needs.

DAY 71

*"At fifteen life had taught me undeniably that sur-
render in its place was as honorable as resistance,
especially if one had no choice."*

—**MAYA ANGELOU**

SURRENDER

Hi Writers,

How often do we live life as though we had all the time in the world,
making choices and avoiding opportunities out of fear? We tell
ourselves that we can do it tomorrow. Confronting our inevitable
demise is not something that particularly appeals to us. In fact, it
probably terrifies most of us.

Our hero is going to die. Not in the physical sense perhaps,
but in a sense that is just as real. Our hero is going to experience a
death of his old identity. He is close to recognizing that what he has
been in search of is impossible to achieve.

Our hero set out on his journey, it got pretty rough and he
suffered, but damn it, he persevered...only to lead to this?

In our own life, have we ever thought, "If I don't get this
thing that I want, my life will not be worth living"?

And then we didn't get it.

We stared into the yawning void. We got those requisite
chills up our spine and then a week, or a month, or twenty years
later, we looked back and thought, "Wow, I survived. I'm stronger
than I thought I was."

For some reason, the simple awareness of this process doesn't seem to matter. It appears that we cannot simply hop over this step and write about it from a detached place—not if we are going to write our story with any specificity. Merely understanding doesn't seem to be worth much. As writers, it seems we are required to experience it, at least on some level.

My brother is a businessman and he told me he doesn't invest in someone's business unless the guy has some *skin in the game*. He wants to know that his partners have something at stake; otherwise, it is too easy for him to pack it up when the going gets tough. As writers, we must have some skin in the game. If we are not invested in our hero's surrender, the moment will lack gravity.

As we grow as writers, we become more comfortable with plunging into the unknown. We know that on the other side of our hero's surrender is a gift.

Until tomorrow,
Al

what if W. tells live story?

WEEK 11: THOUGHTS AND REMINDERS

- Suffering is the final gasp that leads our hero to his moment of surrender.

- We surrender only when we recognize the impossibility of ever getting what we want.

- When our hero surrenders, he reframes his idea of what he wants.

- Until the hero surrenders and reframes his relationship to his goal, there can never be a transformation.

- Our story asks everything of us for a reason. If it didn't, we would never surrender our fixed ideas about ourselves and our world.

- There is a difference between our hero's surrender at the end of Act Two and the battle scene at the end of Act Three. Our hero surrenders because he has no choice. The battle scene involves our hero making a choice. Our hero makes a new choice at the end, thus proving to the gods that he has earned his shift in perception.

HOMEWORK FOR THE WEEK

1. Write a quick point-form outline to the end of Act Two.

2. Write to the moment where the hero surrenders.

DAY 72

"A problem cannot be solved at the same level of consciousness that created it."   —**ALBERT EINSTEIN**

MAKING THE IMPOSSIBLE POSSIBLE

Hi Writers,

We often have an idea of the direction in which our story is headed. Sometimes it does head in that direction, but not in the way we expected. A scene can take a detour and we allow that to happen. We must always be willing to let our characters surprise us.

To some degree, we are embodying our hero's journey. How can we not? This is part of what makes the process so thrilling. We are invested. On some level, we are exploring our own lives and making meaning out of what we discover.

This is important to remember as we approach this stage in our story, because the urgent need that initially roused us is now coming up for review. We are being invited to question all that we have come to believe about what our hero wants.

Fears may naturally arise here. The challenge is to remain curious while not making meaning out of them like we did before. Remember, we have an ace in the hole. We have imagined our hero transformed. We understand that what we had made meaning out of was not the whole truth. It did not include grace. It did not include the possibility for something greater, for something perhaps even beyond our imagination. It did not include a shift in perception. This is the magic of story.

Talking about surrender is like talking about sex; until you've experienced it, it doesn't really mean anything. In the moment of surrender, our hero glimpses the impossibility of getting what he wants. We must investigate the pain and be really specific. Can we remain curious as we witness the death of our hero's identity? It seems impossible, doesn't it? In fact, I believe it is until I understand that I am merely a channel. It is my higher self that steers the ship from here. My higher self guides me, reminding me that from here on in I am in uncharted territory, and yet all that I need is within.

Armed with this knowledge, I am willing to let the old self die, with all of those old, limiting ideas. I don't do this to puff myself up and relive the pattern over again. I cannot fight my antagonist anymore, at least not in the way I have been. I surrender. My way has proven ineffective. There is no hope of winning. In fact, I have come to understand that there is nothing to win. Sometimes our hero needs to experience loss, to drop the old paradigm of winning and losing in order to turn his attention to the truth of his life.

Is this impossible to do? Yes. So we are not going to do it. We are going to let our higher selves do it for us.

Our higher self is that place in us that knows all. He is the wise man on the hill, the large-hearted artist who gazes down at our little drama and offers us a wider perspective.

Until tomorrow,
Al

DAY 73

"Sorrow makes us all children again—destroys all differences of intellect. The wisest knows nothing."
—RALPH WALDO EMERSON

MORE ON SURRENDER

Hi Writers,

This week is all about our hero confronting the impossibility of getting what he wants. This realization can be a despairing moment, but it's often followed by a new awareness that offers hope.

Let's be curious about what this moment looks like. There is a world of difference between what is difficult and what is impossible, between suffering and surrender. The moment of surrender occurs when our hero becomes aware, possibly for the first time, of the true nature of his problem. Remember that our story begins with a problem that is impossible to solve. If it weren't impossible there would be no reason for our hero to surrender.

Surrender does not mean that our hero stops wanting. It means that he recognizes that his desire is creating his pain. In surrendering, he reframes his relationship to what he wants and his perspective widens. He begins to recognize what he needs.

What does our hero need? When we flip the want, we get the need. For example, "Joe wants a motorbike because he thinks it will make him popular." By exploring the *nature* of what it means to be popular, we begin to discover what Joe needs.

- Surrender does not mean giving up.

- Surrender happens when we run out of choices.

- Surrender is the moment we realize it is more painful to hold on than it is to let go.

- Surrender means that we reframe our goal.

- Surrender can feel like our heart is breaking.

- Surrender is the death of our old identity.

- Surrender is the end of an old idea.

- Surrender is the gateway to reality.

- Surrender is the beginning of the ending.

- Surrender is where our perspective widens; it allows us to understand what we were avoiding.

Until tomorrow,
Al

DAY 74

"Beware the person with nothing to lose."
—**ITALIAN PROVERB**

NOTHING TO LOSE

Hi Writers,

As we approach the end of Act Two, let's be curious about the event that causes our hero to surrender. It is through surrendering that our hero accepts the reality of his situation. This often involves a revelation, a sudden understanding of the true nature of his situation.

This bedrock understanding compels our hero to move forward in a more clear-headed way. As he sees how he has been living, it is apparent there is still much to do. The path may be unclear, but having surrendered, he has entered the realm of *anything is possible.*

In *American Beauty*, Lester Burnham blackmails his boss and is told, "You're insane."

He replies, "No, I'm just a guy with nothing to lose."

Let's explore the lengths to which our hero is willing to go when he has nothing to lose.

Until tomorrow,
Al

handwritten note in margin

DAY 75

"If you are going to make a book end badly, it must end badly from the beginning."

—ROBERT LOUIS STEVENSON

TRANSFORMATION

Hi Writers,

A fundamental understanding of transformation is crucial to developing a relationship with structure beyond the theoretical. Many books have been written on three-act structure, yet no one has been able to isolate the transcendent beauty that lies at the heart of every great story. It is one thing to analyze the anatomy of a story, but is it possible that story also contains magic, some ineffable quality that rises from a source we can't explain?

Our job is to track the beats in a compelling and believable way that will lead to a transformation. We cannot do this through intellectual willpower. We must accept that we are co-creators, that our story, in its entirety, is already fully alive in our imagination. It is through cultivating a spirit of curiosity in the face of our doubt that our story is born.

The word transformation can connote a miraculous event. However, transformation is simply a shift in perception. That's it. Nothing more. And yet, when we have seen something one way our entire life and then, in an instant, we see it differently, it can seem miraculous. When a transformation occurs, tension vanishes. Through his journey, the protagonist comes to understand something that he did not previously.

Every story begins with a problem. Our challenge as writers is to understand that our hero wants something and that the stakes are life and death. If our hero does not get what he wants, his life will be unimaginable. If the stakes are any lower, the reader will not care.

Surrendering does not mean giving up what he wants; it means letting go of the meaning he's attached to having it. Transformation occurs when he recognizes, on a fundamental level, that merely getting what he wants is not going to solve his problem. Can you imagine if at the end of *It's A Wonderful Life*, Jimmy Stewart finally left Bedford Falls without realizing that he already had a wonderful life?

We are interested in whether or not the hero is going to get what he needs. When he gives himself what he needs, it becomes possible to have what he wants if it happens to belong in his life.

Until tomorrow,
Al

DAY 76

"Coincidence is the word we use when we can't see the levers and the pulleys."   —EMMA BULL

WE ARE NOT DOING THIS ALONE

Hi Writers,

When we write under a time constraint, we become highly attuned to our environment. We begin asking ourselves, "Where does this live in the world of my story?"

You may have noticed that something else happens. As we write, coincidences seem to arrive out of the blue at just the right time. I have seen it too often not to believe it. We are not doing this alone.

We are writing up to the point where our hero surrenders. This part of the process can invite panic. Our hero surrenders as a result of recognizing the impossibility of getting what he wants. This recognition happens through conflict; without worthy antagonists, there can be no surrender. It is human nature to want to avoid conflict. As writers, our job is to embrace it. Surrender leads us to our story's resolution.

Something interesting often happens as we near the end of Act Two. We begin to understand Act One more clearly. We begin to see what is missing or unclear. We could not have arrived at these insights had we not kept writing. If we had remained in our first act, we would have ended up "perfecting" material that might never have made it to the second draft. This is why we must keep going. However, first, let's make note of these insights. Scribble them down and keep them on file. And don't ever feel beholden to something you wrote in Act One if it is no longer making sense. If it becomes clear that your hero is a pilot and not a surgeon, make him a pilot—then keep going!

Until tomorrow,
Al

DAY 77

*"Sometimes we have to go a long way out of our way
in order to come back a short distance correctly."*
—EDWARD ALBEE ("THE ZOO STORY")

THE BEGINNING OF THE END

Hi Writers,

The end of Act Two is an exhausting place to be. To some degree, we are our hero, and as she approaches her dark night of the soul, so do we. There's a saying: "If you're walking through hell, keep walking." It is through surrendering that our hero is empowered. In reframing her relationship to her goal, the reality of her situation emerges. The beginning of Act Three brings new hope. It is not the hope of getting what she wants, but rather getting what she needs.

In Suzanne Collin's novel *The Hunger Games,* the heroine, Katniss Everdeen, believes that love is a sham that will only lead to heartache. She does not trust Peeta's overtures, which she suspects are only a ruse to gain advantage over her. By the end of the story she has experienced his unconditional love for her.

It is at the end of Act Two/beginning of Act Three that our hero reframes her relationship to her old belief. She begins to wake up to the reality of her situation. Her perspective widens and new possibilities emerge.

It's more important to be curious about the shift rather than to nail it in the first draft. Let's be gentle with ourselves here.

Writing a story is a war of attrition. Oftentimes we inch toward our hero's transformation.

Until tomorrow,
Al

WEEK 12

ACT THREE:
OUR HERO TAKES ACTION

Through surrendering his old relationship to his goal, our hero develops wisdom. He begins to accept the reality of his situation and is able to give himself what he needs. This week, our hero may encounter situations with antagonists, but his approach is shifting, informed by a new understanding.

DAY 78

"In the attitude of silence, the soul finds the path in a clearer light, and what is elusive and deceptive resolves itself into crystal clearness. Our life is a long and arduous quest after Truth."

—Mahatma Gandhi

REFRAMING THE WANT

Hi Writers,

This week we begin writing our third act. In Act Three, our hero accepts the reality of his situation. He stops fighting a battle that he can't win. Be curious about how your hero reframes his want. In *It's A Wonderful Life*, Clarence appears just as ol' Jimmy is about to jump into an icy river to end his life. Clarence is not only a character but also the device that literally reframes Jimmy's relationship to what he wants. When the hero lets go of his initial goal, he can begin to understand what he actually needs. If you're feeling stuck, take a look at what has happened in the Second Act and be curious about what needs to happen in order to resolve these relationships.

Until tomorrow,
Al

WEEK 12: THOUGHTS AND REMINDERS

- Act Three often begins with a gift of sorts, even if it is just a new understanding of the situation.

- The hero often begins to understand the nature of his dilemma at the beginning of Act Three. He may begin to understand that what he wanted was actually impossible to achieve, at least in light of where he was coming from.

- Act Three involves the hero accepting the reality of his situation, taking action, and finally, making a new choice.

- When we are struggling with our story, it can be helpful to inquire into the nature of our struggle. This is often where our story problem lies. Example: If I can't see how my hero will ever experience liberation from his problem, it might be helpful to explore the expectations I have for my completed novel. If I expect my writing to relieve me of a life of boredom or to allow me to quit a job I despise, then perhaps I can recognize a parallel between myself and my hero. What would it look like if I accepted the possibility that this job I consider unimaginable was, in fact, tolerable? What if my hero understood that acceptance did not mean weak resignation, but rather a willingness to accept things as they are?

- The goal of the first draft is simply to get to the end of the story.

HOMEWORK FOR THE WEEK

1. Write a quick point-form outline of Act Three.

2. Find a point midway through Act Three and write to that point.

DAY 79

"You never find yourself until you face the truth."
—Pearl Bailey

ACCEPTING REALITY

Hi Writers,

Our story is bigger than we are. In fact, it does not even belong to us. We are simply a channel. If you are beginning to panic and think, "I don't have a third act," relax. Everything we need to know is within us.

The desire to write a story is a setup. We begin with excitement only to realize that our story has asked everything of us. This story is coming from somewhere deep down, somewhere primal, and it is not going to settle for mere survival. It wants more.

Sometimes we think, God, just get me through this day, or month, or life. We just want to survive. It can be frightening to ask *what if*, to inquire into the possibility of real freedom.

But asking "what if" is the stuff of great fiction. Asking "what if" is the stuff of Act Three. What if we allowed our idea of our story to collapse? What if we accepted that we just didn't know? Wouldn't we be exactly where our hero is? And how would that alter our perception? Well, hasn't our hero spent the entire story pursuing his idea of how he thinks things should go? And how has that been working? It hasn't.

In Act Three, a paradigm shift occurs. The challenge is that we must trust in our hero's transformation, even if we don't know precisely how it will play out. Sounds like life, doesn't it? We must bypass all of our conditioning, everything that we believed made us safe, and trust in that childlike place where we are naturally moved by the truth of our story.

This is not weak sentimentality. I am not talking about manipulation or tugging at the heartstrings of our reader, but I am talking about love, that mysterious thing that lies at the heart of every story. Despite the tone or the genre, love is always on the table and it behooves us to investigate into the nature of the love, or lack of it, that exists between our characters. Investigating into the nature of love makes our story specific and lifts it beyond the realm of idea.

It might also be helpful to explore our own relationship to love. What beliefs have we accepted without questioning that are now hindering us from allowing our hero to grow?

As we do this, ideas may occur to us that begin to reveal an ending. We will know the ending is right because it rings like a bell. We have found some kind of order in the chaos. Our hero has been returned home.

Until tomorrow,
Al

DAY 80

"There is nothing in a caterpillar that tells you it's going to be a butterfly."
—R. BUCKMINSTER FULLER

SURRENDERING CONTROL

Hi Writers,

In Act Three our hero accepts the reality of his situation. How do we know what that reality is? We simply imagine our hero transformed. Our imagination can instantly transcend our old level of consciousness. We have an unlimited capacity to evolve. Our only job seems to be envisioning what seems impossible and imagining its possibility.

We imagine our hero freed from his dilemma, the tension that's been driving him, and we are curious about how this experience alters his relationships to other characters in the story. It doesn't mean that the characters are suddenly getting along, for instance. It may just mean that our hero is no longer holding onto his old ideas about how things ought to be.

When we have a sense of our hero transformed, we have a place to write to. We can go back to the beginning of Act Three and track our story from that place. Our hero has a lot of work to do to get to the place of true understanding. Let's be curious about the moments that lead to this place. This is the content of Act Three.

If you're anything like me, you want to control everything,

the pain, the joy . . . everything. Act Three is about leaving the familiar. It's the hero's desire for control that perpetuates his failure to achieve his goal. The idea our hero clings to must be surrendered. His true identity is indestructible. It exists separate from all of his ideas about himself. This is the place our hero visits in the battle scene. This is the place to which our hero is returned home.

Until tomorrow,
Al

DAY 81

"Finishing a book is just like you took a child out in the backyard and shot it."   —Truman Capote

WHY ARE WE FINISHING OUR BOOK?

Hi Writers,

As we approach the end of our first draft we may experience doubt. We may start to ask the big existential questions or ponder why we ought to bother finishing when wars are being fought and people are starving and families are being torn apart. Who is going to care about our little story?

We can be pulled into all sorts of psychic spirals that are intent on one thing: preventing us from getting to the end. It doesn't really matter why. Fear is fear. Just as our hero reframes his relationship to his goal in order to make the impossible possible, we must do the same. The reason we began this thing might not get us to the end. We may need to reframe it.

Why are we finishing our book? Because we started it. Because we are writers now and our job is to build a body of work.

Our reasons for quitting can be convincing. They can also be vague. The thrill of creation must be its own reward. We are close. Let's steel ourselves. Let's show up on the page each day. Let's give ourselves permission to write poorly. Let's get to the end.

Until tomorrow,
Al

DAY 82

"Hunger, love, pain, fear are some of those inner forces which rule the individual's instinct for survival."
—**ALBERT EINSTEIN**

PRIMAL

Hi Writers,

Primal desires drive our characters. We are all motivated by hunger, fear, lust, ambition, freedom, revenge. A primal desire for our hero provides our story with a through-line. A primal response is related to a character's desires and not his feelings. Our reader is not particularly interested in our characters' feelings. If our hero is going to find his way home, we must not become lost in the largeness of our feelings. Who knows what a panther feels as it stalks its prey? All that matters is that it must kill to survive. Leave the reader to have an emotional experience. Our job is to explore our hero's attempts at achieving his goal.

Sometimes we have a tendency to bolster a character's motive by adding more than one reason for an action. This can actually be confusing and, in fact, weaken the motive. When we have more than one reason for a motive, it might be a sign that we're not connected to our hero's primal drive. Make it specific.

Until tomorrow,
Al

DAY 83

"Without humility there can be no humanity."
—JOHN BUCHAN

THE HERO STRIPPED BARE

Hi Writers,

In Act Three we are paying off everything that we have set up throughout the story. Our hero has been stripped bare in order to understand the reality of her situation. It becomes clear that her apparent problem is in fact a dilemma. *The Hunger Games* begins with the problem of survival, but as the story progresses, Katniss begins to face a dilemma. The question of survival collides with the question of trust. Is it possible that Peeta would actually be willing to die for her or is he pretending and does he intend to kill her? Though the dramatic question may be, "Will Katniss survive?" it is the underlying question, "Does love really exist?" that keeps us turning the page.

Act Three pays off the dramatic question. Let's keep our hero moving, making choices and confronting obstacles that will lead to the final battle scene.

The battle scene is internal. The hero's choice is difficult. It often involves what appears to be a sacrifice, like letting go of something she thought she valued, which may, in fact, just have been an old belief that no longer serves her. In Katniss' case, it could be this question of survival. She has lived her life with her head down, scrounging for food and not allowing herself to entertain the possibility of love.

In proving to the gods that our hero has earned her transformation, she must be willing to make a new choice. In the case of Katniss Everdeen, her final battle is the struggle in her own heart: will she love or will she return to simply surviving?

What is the choice that your hero makes? If you're not sure, investigate the disparity between what she *wants* and what she *needs*. Be curious about the images that arise when you imagine these two forces in conflict with each other. This will lead you to your hero's final choice.

Until tomorrow,
Al

DAY 84

"Trust one who has gone through it."
—VIRGIL (THE AENEID)

HOW DO I WRITE MY ENDING?

Hi Writers,

In Act Three, our hero accepts the possibility that he will never get what he wants and begins to accept the reality of his situation. In doing so, he takes action and begins to consider what he needs.

If we really knew, or were able to accept what we needed, perhaps we wouldn't spend so much time running away from it. Remember, our idea of the story was never the whole story, because we make meaning out of our past. This meaning leads to a false belief. The battle scene is our hero's opportunity to make a new choice, thus illustrating a new belief. When we imagine our hero transformed, our subconscious begins to find a through-line to that place. And that is the solution to our ending. The hero's problem could not be solved in the past because his true problem was an unwillingness or inability to accept the reality of his situation.

Once our hero gives himself what he needs, the dilemma resolves itself. That doesn't mean he no longer wants what he wants, it just no longer rules him because he recognizes the danger of putting his desires before his needs.

Let's be curious about what our hero needs. What does it look like? We don't have to solve it right now. This is just our first draft. We are allowing it to be as raw and alive as it wants to be and we are staying out of the result.

Until tomorrow,
Al

DAY 85

"The rule of the writer is not to say what we can all say, but what we are unable to say."

—ANAÏS NIN

THE BATTLE SCENE

Hi Writers,

We are approaching the battle scene in our story. This is the climax. The hero makes a new choice, thus proving to the gods that he has earned his transformation. He understands his world in a new way.

The battle is internal for our hero, although it may manifest itself externally. The hero's choice is difficult; it's a battle he wages against himself. Ultimately we are our greatest antagonist. The outer manifestations of drama were merely tests to lead us to this moment of choice. What will we choose? This can be tricky. The novice may, at this moment, want to plant his flag and shout to the world that war is bad or that evil must be eradicated. But dogmatic effusions will leave our reader unmoved. The power of story rests in the writer's ability to present a convincing counterargument that leads to a deeper truth. This is not something that can be consciously figured out because our story was never really about war or evil. It was about the struggle of our hero to accept the reality of his situation. That is what every story is about, and the events of the plot are merely a vehicle to bring our hero to this place of choice. The choice is between what our hero wants and what he needs. It often involves what appears to be a sacrifice, e.g., letting go of something he thought he valued, which may, in fact, have just been an old idea that no longer serves him. Will he choose security or freedom? Money or love? Belonging or integrity? Will he proclaim his truth and lose something he previously valued, or will he choose the easier path?

We must trust that somewhere within us lies the truth. This truth lives beyond our ego, beyond our preconceived ideas of the world, and beyond everything we have been told is true. This truth is anarchic. It cares more about the nature of things than our own security or sense of belonging. When we tap into this truth, everything changes.

Until tomorrow,
Al

THE ENDING

ACT THREE:
OUR HERO RETURNS HOME

But first he must prove to the gods that he has earned his *transformation*. This week our hero will make a choice between what he wants and what he needs. The paradox of Act Three is that in surrendering his goal, it becomes possible for him to achieve it if it belongs in his life. In making this final choice, our hero is returned home.

DAY 86

"We are all faced with a series of great opportunities
brilliantly disguised as impossible situations."
—CHARLES R. SWINDOLL

DEUS EX MACHINA

Hi Writers,

Deus ex machina is Latin for "god out of the machine." It refers to endings in which a seemingly intractable problem is solved by the introduction of a new character, or a sudden event happens out of the blue that neatly ties up the story. These endings leave readers unsatisfied. The ending is the completion of a theme and its seed can be found in the beginning.

A satisfying ending fulfills two criteria. It is, to some degree, a surprise while also being utterly inevitable; in retrospect, it could not have ended any other way.

The Lovely Bones is a wonderful book with a deus ex machina moment when George Harvey, the villain who rapes and kills Susie Salmon, is killed by an icicle falling on his head. There is an implication that Susie, by some force of will, has orchestrated this from heaven. It's a convenient way to get rid of the bad guy but it comes from out of nowhere and breaks the rules of the world that has been created.

If you are struggling with your ending, look to your beginning. What are you trying to say? What is resolved at the end of the story? You don't have to figure it out; just remain open to what you're attempting to express and be curious about what the story wants to tell you. Sometimes we discover these things as we're writing them.

This week:

- I will be specific.

- I will be open to whatever wants to happen in my story even if it appears to be in opposition to where I thought my story was heading.

- Even though I know what will happen, I may be surprised by how it happens.

- I know that although my hero makes a difficult choice during the battle, afterwards it seems like the most obvious choice in the world.

- I am not doing this alone. I am being guided. All I have to do is drop everything I think I know in order to allow the truth to emerge.

- I trust there is an underlying truth in the story that lives within me, even if I am not yet clear on what it is.

- The battle scene may be bittersweet, but it is not a compromise.

- I cannot make a mistake. All I need to do is continue to inquire.

- I just need to get to the end.

- I can fix it in the rewrite.

Until tomorrow,
Al

OUR HERO RETURNS HOME: THOUGHTS AND REMINDERS

- The dilemma is resolved during the battle scene.

- The hero proves to the gods that he has earned his transformation during the battle scene.

- The battle scene involves a choice for the hero. Make it active.

- "Active" does not necessarily mean "external." It can be an internal shift.

- The hero makes a choice between what he wants and what he needs during the battle scene.

- The battle scene is just that, a battle. It is a difficult choice. If it was easy, the reader wouldn't care. The hero is invested. What is he going to choose?

- A satisfying ending to a story is a total surprise, and yet it is utterly inevitable. It could not have ended any other way. The seed of the ending was planted in the beginning.

- Our hero's want and need collide in the battle scene. Perhaps there is a situation where he must choose to behave in a way that a person who was complete might behave. Perhaps he does not make a choice out of desperation or self-loathing.

- What does your hero come to understand as the result of his journey?

- Our hero is returned home. What does this new equilibrium look like?

HOMEWORK:

1. Write a quick point-form outline to the end of your novel.

2. Write to the end of the first draft of your novel.

DAY 87

" 'When you realize the story you're telling is just
words, when you can just crumble it up and throw
your past in the trashcan,' Brandy says, 'then we'll
figure out who you're going to be.' "

—**CHUCK PALHANIUK** (*Invisible Monsters*)

STORY IS AN INSIDE JOB/CHOICE

Hi Writers,

Our story is an inside job. If we're feeling uncertain about our battle
scene, all we have to do is imagine our hero transformed. We are
developing a relationship to our hero at the end of the story and it
is out of this that our battle scene emerges. Images or situations will
come to us as we imagine our hero confronting his choice between
getting what he wants and getting what he needs.

In Charlotte Bronte's novel *Jane Eyre,* the title character
experiences despair when her marriage to Rochester is foiled by
unforeseen circumstances. Before she is able to find happiness with
the love of her life, her strength is tested by years of hardship. Toward the end of the story, she considers marrying another man, St.
John, and must decide between a life on her own and a stable loveless marriage. She chooses to be alone, proving to the gods that she
is no longer a girl dependent on others, and in doing so is returned
to Rochester.

It is our hero's choice that reveals the underlying meaning

we have set up throughout the story. Everything has been leading to this moment. Our hero's choice resolves the dilemma. In Ibsen's play "An Enemy of the People," Dr. Thomas Stockmann alerts the townsfolk that their water supply is contaminated and potentially deadly. The townsfolk despise him for wanting to make this public, bringing potential ruin to the town. He is confronted with the choice of remaining silent or standing up for the truth, even if it means risking the lives of his family. He chooses the truth, a difficult decision, and yet the moment the choice is made, it seems quite inevitable.

Whether it is Jane Eyre choosing a hard and lonely life over a loveless marriage or Dr. Stockmann risking potential death in order to spread a disturbing truth, story is a means of connecting us to our highest selves.

There can be a tendency to intellectualize this process. If you're feeling stuck, give yourselves permission to ignore everything I have said, trust your gut, and write to the end. The only thing that matters is that our stories live. Be willing to surprise yourselves even if it appears that the story is going to collapse in contradiction. We can always revisit it in the rewrite. We may discover that when we explore the direction the story is pulling us, we will come out the other end with a conclusion that is both surprising and utterly inevitable.

Until tomorrow,
Al

DAY 88

*"The opposite of a correct statement is a false state-
ment. But the opposite of a profound truth may well
be another profound truth."*   —NIELS BOHR

WHAT OUR HERO KNOWS TO BE TRUE

Hi Writers,

Our hero must go on a journey in order to discover what he always
knew to be true. What has he been resisting? Let's be curious about
what our hero's life looks like when he accepts this truth. We don't
have to like something in order to accept it. For example, one day
we are going to die. Sorry if you're hearing this for the first time.
This is not good news but it is often in accepting the finite nature
of existence that we make productive choices, because the pain of
not living life fully is greater than letting it pass us by. How does
our hero choose life?

     What our hero knows to be true is a synthesis of two seem-
ingly disparate beliefs. "Love conquers all" versus "no one is to be
trusted," "hard work is rewarded" versus "the world is basically un-
fair." It is through the drama of Act Three that our hero arrives at a
synthesis of two opposing ideas to reveal a deeper truth. In learning
to trust himself, he finds love. In reframing his ideas on fairness, he
feels valued for his hard work.

     Two more days. Act Three will inevitably have some holes
in it. That's okay. It just means that our story has some breathing

room. As we get more specific in the rewrite these holes will get filled in.

Until tomorrow,
Al

DAY 89

"Meaning is not something you stumble across, like the answer to a riddle or the prize in a treasure hunt. Meaning is something you build into your life."
—JOHN GARDNER

OUR HERO RETURNS HOME

Hi Writers,

The ending of our story is about a new understanding. How is our hero relating differently to the other characters in his world? Sometimes when we are exhausted and have no more fight left in us, we are paradoxically at our most powerful. We don't have the breath to defend our position. Things that used to matter no longer seem important. We are grateful for life's smallest niceties. When we stop running our game, we may discover that what we had been attempting to protect did not need protecting and in fact was preventing us from getting what we wanted. Through our hero's journey, perhaps he comes to understand a new truth and gains a wider perspective. Perhaps freedom was nothing more than letting go of an old idea.

In story, the whole is greater than the sum of its parts. Our elegant prose, witty rejoinders, stunning insights and galloping narrative are all in service to one thing—a larger meaning. What is our story about? What are we attempting to express? This is the moment when our story comes together. Our hero arrives at a new understanding.

When I wrote the first draft of *Diamond Dogs*, I woke up on the morning I was to write the story's climax, the confrontation between the father and the son, and I was stuck. Completely blank. Paralyzed. Every morning I had begun my writing with a prayer to the gods to guide my pen, but on this day my prayers went unanswered. I had a sense of what was supposed to happen, but I couldn't write it. I began scribbling in my journal, cursing God. Finally, I stood up from my desk, threw open my door, and ordered Him out of my hotel room. I sat down and blasted out eight pages in an hour. I was on fire. I didn't care if I lived or died. I was going to finish this book and I was going to leave it all on the page.

I wrote the climax and then set down my pen. I stared out the window at the afternoon traffic. I felt a freedom unlike anything I'd ever experienced. There was this strange sensation as I sat on the couch, like I was not alone. I blinked.

"You didn't leave, did you?" I said to this presence with which I had become so familiar. The response was immediate. "No," it said to me, "That was your father."

At times, writing is liberating; at other times, it is an exorcism. Regardless, our muse never leaves us. We may become temporarily panicked and lose our connection, but if we stay with it, worlds will move.

Keep going.

Until tomorrow,
Al

DAY 90

"If the foot of the trees were not tied to the earth, they would be pursuing me . . . for I have blossomed so much, I am the envy of the gardens."   —RUMI

THE ENDING

Hi Writers,

We're not done yet. Today we write our ending, and as we write, let's ask ourselves some questions.

- Have I said all I set out to say?
- Have I satisfied all the questions my reader may have?
- Have I resolved any and all loose ends with my characters?

And finally, how am I going to end this thing . . . specifically? Is my ending a surprise, and yet utterly inevitable? If not, what can I do to make it so. Is it possible, perhaps, to make a connection between the beginning of my story and the ending? Can I find a way to show the vastness of my protagonist's journey? Is there an image, an idea, or a theme that can bring my story full circle? How do I resolve the dilemma at the heart of the story and return my hero home?

Although the ending is the "falling action" the author still has some tricks up her sleeve. She isn't finished yet. The ending is about clarifying what we have been attempting to express.

Story accumulates meaning as it progresses, leading inexorably to its final moment when all is made clear. Even if our ending is ambiguous, open-ended, or existential—let's never confuse this with being general.

What do we want our reader to know? How can we show it?

Okay. Now write it down quickly, and don't worry about the prose. Say it all. Don't hold anything back. Leave it all on the page. This is your moment.

Write! Now! Go!

Congratulations! You did it!

Today is an auspicious day, and a day like any other. Today we show up for our writing because we are writers. Today we write the words *The End* on the first drafts of our novels. Writing is a courageous act. Is it possible that the purpose of writing our novel, whether or not it becomes an award-winning bestseller, is to express our truth on the page? If our sole reason for writing this book had been to sell it for a million dollars or to impress our parents we would probably not have gotten this far. We got to the end because we discovered that the thrill of creation is its own reward.

One final thought. I believe we cannot grow as artists without a generous spirit. The reason *why* we write is at least as important as *what* we write. Our creative work does not belong to us. It's a function of our consciousness—it passes through us and we are merely documenting its birth. When we write with no expectation of return we connect to a universal principle that lies at the core of the creative impulse. Perhaps what is called talent is nothing more than a willingness to remain curious in the face of doubt and document what arises. I've heard it said that writing can't be taught, and on some level this may be true. We can teach principles of story, and we can illustrate a process, but these fundamentals are useless without an open heart. It took me years to understand this, and I suppose we teach what we most need to learn. By nurturing a generous spirit we are actively practicing surrender, patience, curiosity and faith: vital tools for a writer's life.

I'm truly thrilled for you, and honored that you took the trip. When your book comes out, make sure you invite me to the reading. Just send me an email at al@the90daynovel.com and I will put the word out on my website.

Now go celebrate. Tomorrow we start the rewrite.

Your fellow writer,
Al

PART THREE

the 90-day novel

STREAM-OF-CONSCIOUSNESS WRITING EXERCISES

S tory is primal. The stakes are life and death for our characters. These writing exercises are meant to spark your imagination and get your characters speaking to you. The story
lives within. We don't need to figure it out. As you write stream-of-
consciousness for five minutes on any of these questions, a sense of
the world of your story will begin to emerge. After a short while,
whether it is a few days or a week, begin to incorporate the structure questions into this work of imagining the world of your story.
The structure questions invite up images at various stages in the
hero's journey. By working with them, they will help you to develop
an outline for your story.

From the perspective of your hero or an antagonist, write
for five minutes, beginning with the following line:

1. One thing you still need to know about me is . . .

2. The lie I continually tell myself is . . .

3. What makes me angry is . . .

4. What breaks my heart is . . .

5. The secret I won't tell anyone is . . .

6. The secret I won't tell myself is . . .

7. My perfect day would be . . .

8. This is how I would spend my last day on earth . . .

9. The biggest shock of my life was when . . .

10. I feel trapped when . . .

11. My first love was . . .

12. My biggest regret was . . .

13. My greatest accomplishment has been . . .

14. My childhood dream was . . .

15. When I look in the mirror, I see . . .

16. If you knew me before, you would have said . . .

17. Tomorrow I am going to . . .

18. On my tombstone, it will read . . .

19. On my tombstone, I would like it to read . . .

20. What I have come to understand is . . .

21. I fear that when people look at me they see . . .

22. The person I hate the most is . . .

23. You would never know this by looking at me, but . . .

24. My secret love is . . .

25. I can't wait for . . .

26. My attitude toward sex is . . .

27. My philosophy on life is . . .

28. I believe my role in life is to . . .

29. My favorite thing to do is . . .

30. The thought that keeps me up at night is . . .

31. One day I am going to . . .

32. I feel free when . . .

33. The best thing I ever purchased was . . .

34. My favorite memory is . . .

35. My worst memory is . . .

36. When I want to comfort myself I remember . . .

37. The closest I ever came to murder was when . . .

38. The place I go when I don't want anyone to find me is . . .

39. If you were to ask the closest person in my life who I am, (and they were to tell the truth) they would say . . .

40. I would be crushed if anyone knew that . . .

41. The one thing I care most about is . . .

42. I used to believe that . . .

43. The truth about myself that I'm resisting is . . .

44. The truth I'm resisting in my story is . . .

45. Every time I think I'm going to get what I want, it seems that . . .

46. When I wake up my first thought is . . .

47. My last thought before I fall asleep is . . .

48. I have a habit of . . .

49. The answer to my problem that I've been avoiding is . . .

50. My worst defeat was when . . .

51. I will finally rest when . . .

52. The bravest thing I've ever done is . . .

53. The most cowardly thing I've ever done is . . .

54. My relationship to God is . . .

55. The defining moment of my life was when . . .

56. The greatest love of my life is . . .

57. The last time I remember laughing hard was when . . .

58. The one thing I could never survive is . . .

59. The greatest thrill of my life was when . . .

60. My most painful memory is . . .

61. I need to be forgiven for . . .

62. If I could do one thing differently from my past, it would be . . .

63. The message I got from my father was . . .

64. The message I got from my mother was . . .

65. The reason I'm in this situation is because . . .

66. If I were to tell the truth, the consequence would be . . .

67. I believe that . . . (as your hero at the beginning of the story)

68. I know it to be true that . . . (as your hero at the end of the story)

69. To me, freedom looks like . . .

70. Something I expect from others is . . .

71. Something I expect from myself is . . .

72. Write a dialogue between your hero and an antagonist. The hero wants something, and the antagonist is unwilling to give it to him. Play this out until one of them succeeds (or dies trying).

THE STRUCTURE QUESTIONS

The structure questions are written in order and are the key plot points in our hero's journey. We inquire repeatedly into these questions, and simply write down whatever images appear. We are not answering these questions in the traditional sense. We are inquiring into our protagonist at various stages in his journey, as the loosest sense of a story begins to appear. Story structure is not a formula. If you find yourself balking at these questions, feel free to disregard them. Story structure is so often taught as a formula that it's understandable for artists to eschew structure as limiting and reductive. However, I believe these questions can be applied to any story, from the most 'traditionally structured' to the most esoteric piece of writing ever written. By simply inquiring into them, they can lead to a more dynamic vision for our story. If we intellectualize them, however, we will grow frustrated.

When structure is approached in this way, it becomes the single most powerful tool in assuring a narrative drive. Story structure is not about 'plot.' Our characters suggest plot. The structure questions are a way to get underneath the plot and to start tapping into our story's underlying meaning. This is a non-linear process. Images may reveal themselves that seem disconnected from other parts in our emerging story. These questions allow us to move beyond our limited ideas of the story. They ignite our subconscious as it seeks to make order, to track a through-line that allows our hero to move from the beginning to the end. We are marrying the wildness of our imaginations to the rigor of story structure. It is a dance. We can't just snap our fingers and structure our story. This process is about making choices and holding them all loosely. It is a process of constant inquiry as the most dynamic version of our story is revealed.

On Day 22, there is a structural analysis of my novel *Diamond Dogs*, with some thoughts on the process as well.

Write for a few minutes on each of these questions, and be curious about what emerges. Write as fast as you can. Don't approach this like a college exam. Have fun.

ACT ONE

1. OPENING: How does my story begin? What is the initial experience? What images and ideas emerge?

2. THEME: What is the dramatic question, or dilemma in my story? (A dilemma is a problem that cannot be solved without creating another problem. Problems are solved. Dilemmas are resolved through a shift in perception).

3. INCITING INCIDENT: What event happens that sets my story into motion?

4. OPPOSING ARGUMENT: How does my antagonist respond to the hero?

5. END OF ACT ONE: What decision does my hero make that he can't go back on?

ACT TWO

6. FALSE VICTORY: What is the first sign of growth or success that my protagonist experiences toward achieving his goal?

7. MIDPOINT: What event forces my protagonist to respond? This event often involves temptation. He could go back to where he was, or forge into the unknown and risk losing ev-

erything.

8. SUFFERING: What does it look like when my protagonist realizes that this is more difficult than he had imagined? How
does he suffer? *O*

9. <u>Surrender:</u> What would it look like if my hero realized that
what he was pursuing was impossible to achieve?

* Quint returned / knows CB knows the way

ACT THREE

10. REALITY: What is the truth of my hero's reality that he is beginning to accept? *CB knows the way - partial ment. vote to destroy partal. he destroys*

11. ACTION: What action does my hero take as a result of accepting the reality of his situation?

12. CHOICE: What image or event do I imagine when I think of
my hero's want and need colliding, or coming into battle with
each other?

13. HERO RETURNS HOME: What is the final image in my story?

*tries to do it alone –
crew won't let him*

ACKNOWLEDGEMENTS

Thank you to my teachers: To Viki King for reaffirming in me that the story lives in our hearts and not in our heads. Your wisdom, love and generous spirit have infused my work, and I am forever grateful to you. To Allison Burnett for reading everything I write, for your brilliance, insight and sense of humor. I'm so lucky to know you. Thanks to my friend and wild man, professor Eric Miles Williamson, for continually reminding me that if we're not scaring ourselves we're not doing our job. Thank you to all the instructors, guest lecturers and staff who have contributed their time and effort to the LA Writers' Lab workshops, including Aimee Bender, Allison Burnett, Lucinda Clare, Tod Goldberg, Derek Haas, Shelby Hiatt, Viki King, DeLaune Michel, Donna Powers, Andrea Seigel, Benjamin van der Veen, Diana Wagman, Mindi White, Cassie Pappas, Tiffany Gillespie, Diahnna Nicole Baxter, and so many others. Thank you to my agents, Jonathan Lyons at Lyons Literary LLC, and Matthew Snyder at Creative Artists Agency for your smarts, implacable resolve and for continuing to take my calls. Thanks to my lawyers, Ryan Nord and Paul Supnik for doing stuff I don't quite understand.

Thank you to Lisa Hanson for copy-editing this manuscript. I'm grateful for your insights, diligence and professionalism. Thank you to Jenna Lundeen at Lundeen Literary for formatting and troubleshooting—you are a godsend. Thanks to Ryan Basile for the cover art. Thank you to Stephanie Feury and the SFS Theater for hosting our Saturday morning workshops. Thank you to Bret Phillips, Ted Meyer, Kalin Clements and Joe Lackner for developing the websites, graphic design and photography. Thanks to

Aaron Lee, Dr. Steven Dansiger, Eugene Buica, David and Deborah Streit, Staci Cain, Marianne Giblin, Dave Polsky, Tony Vitale, Jeff Gund, Kieran Kennedy, Ben Hunnicutt, Russ Pfeiffer, Jon Reede, Mirna Sanchez, Mark Travis, Jennifer Sagiao, Esther Ting, Bob Thiele, Lara Taubman, Aaron Henne, Jerry and Stephanie Harris, Kim from LA, Roma Maffia, Frank B. Wilderson III, Rebecca de Mornay, the Beverly Hills Public Library, Tim Conlon, Marc and Elaine Zicree, Daniela Hinsch, Fairfax Library, Sandy McDaniel, Jim Lewis, David Liss, Anna Jarota, Aurelion Masson, Stephen Pressfield, Kristen and Eric Welch, Olga Watt, Sandy Watt, Chris Watt, Mike Watt and Vivian Watt for all of your love and support. Thank you to Dr. Thomas Brod, Jack Lee Rosenberg, the UCLA Summer Writing program for giving me my first teaching job, to DeLaune Michel and Spoken Interludes, to Nicolas Duval, Pascal Chameuil, Laurent Zeitoun, and Yann Zenou, and everyone at Quad Films.

And finally, to my wife, Mary-Beth Manning, who for years allowed me to conduct three-hour workshops three nights a week in our dining room. You are a kind and patient creature, and the best decision I ever made.

The following is a preview of

the 90-day rewrite

by
Alan Watt

Coming soon.

Please go to
www.lawriterslab.com
for more details.

AN OVERVIEW OF THE PROCESS

M any writers have struggled for years, even decades, with the same story, and have found that *the 90-Day Novel* process allowed them to get to the end of their first draft. The decision to simply let go of the result and inquire into the nature of our story allows us to tap into an infinite reservoir of new possibilities. When we realize that our initial idea of our story is not the whole story, we make room for a fuller story to emerge.

The 90-Day Rewrite is the continuation of a process that sprang from a single thought. We are seeking to make order from chaos, to understand in a more complete way the underlying nature of whatever holds our curiosity. Our first draft was about getting the story onto the page. We had a sense of a beginning, middle, and end, and we wrote it quickly.

Our story is bigger than we are, and the patterns that support our story's central dilemma could not possibly have been written by us, at least, not by our conscious selves. As we move from the general to the specific in the rewrite, we begin to recognize the patterns our subconscious created quite naturally. They might be recurring themes or images, or the recognition of a new layer of meaning we had not intended, but that we now see as present throughout our entire story and articulates what may previously have been nothing more than a nagging impulse. In short, we begin to notice patterns; seemingly random collisions of themes and ideas that help serve to express something we still may not totally understand. These are the result of a willingness to be a channel for our subconscious. The desire to write is connected to the desire to evolve; in other words, our subconscious was connected to the dilemma at the heart of our story, whether we were aware of it or not.

In the rewrite, our primary concern is to remain connected to that ineffable impulse that has driven us to get this first draft onto the page. If we have gotten this far, it is because our story holds something for us beneath the apparent plot, a dilemma for our hero that begs to be resolved.

The first draft was essentially a right-brain process. The rewrite will utilize both sides of our brain. There will be times when we are analyzing, editing, reordering and layering existing material, while at other times we are engaged in generating new material.

Even as we rewrite, we continue to hold our story loosely. The more we are willing to remain connected to our impulse, that inner urging that 'knows' what feels right and is searching for a fundamental truth, the more inclined we will be to sense when something isn't working, to question why we have written what we have written, and to be open to all sorts of creative solutions. It seems that the more we cling to our idea of our story, the more we tend to choke the life out of it. In the rewrite, we are engaged in a process of continually shedding our ideas of what our story ought to be, for the story that wants to live.

The 90-Day Rewrite is an intensive immersion into a process that will continue past these 90 days, but will arm you with a series of practical tools, as well as a basic approach to story that will enhance your current writing practice. Our goal is simple. We want our story to live. This may sound obvious, but it bears consideration as we approach our rewrite. We don't want to confuse perfection with excellence. Perfection is unattainable, an idea that leads us away from the aliveness of our story, while excellence implies a mastery of craft.

FROM THE GENERAL TO THE SPECIFIC

Our goal is to create a story that captures all of the complexity and paradox of the human experience. In the rewrite it's helpful to have a basic confidence in the arc of our hero's journey, the basic beats that lead to our hero's transformation, before getting into the minutiae - character, dialogue, and the refining of prose.

STAYING CONNECTED TO OUR ORIGINAL IMPULSE

We never want to force our story into our idea of how it ought to be structured. Our original impulse was valid. We can trust it. We can return to it over and over again, even as the story continues to be reshaped. Our stories don't live in our intellect; they live in our imaginations.

We may have a better sense of story structure than we think we do. Sometimes we want to make structure more difficult than it is by trying to figure it out. It seems the art of storytelling involves a willingness to surrender our idea of the way the story should be told, for the way it actually wants to be told. We have probably had the experience that our characters 'just began speaking on their own.' In the rewrite, we are attempting to marry the wildness of our first draft with a more specific sense of structure. We don't ever want to think of story structure as a puzzle to be solved, or as a test to be passed. Our story's structure will ultimately support all of the aliveness our imaginations can conjure. We don't ever have to force it. On the contrary, what is often required is patient and rigorous inquiry.

READ THE FIRST DRAFT

Our first task in the rewrite is to read our first draft. We don't judge it. If we want to make notes, we keep them simple. It can be surprising to discover that we love parts we thought were monotonous, and are bored stiff by sections we thought profound. There may even be whole sections we have no recollection of having written.

Sometimes, in our alpha state, we were not even conscious of what was being written through us.

STRUCTURE: THE ORDER OF EVENTS

In the rewrite we are seeking the most effective and compelling way to reveal our story. This can be daunting as there is inevitably a degree of rigidity in our relationship to our story. We fear that if it is not told precisely as we had imagined it, it won't work.

If we can stay connected to the nature of what we're attempting to express, and trust that this takes precedence, we may notice that our story is actually quite malleable. By remaining open to the possibility of reordering events, conflating characters and scenes, layering material from other scenes, and exploring creative ways to dramatize exposition, our story begins to move in the direction of its intended shape.

A NEW OUTLINE

It's often helpful to begin the second draft with a fresh outline. We now know so much more about our characters and story. This outline is not simply a rehashing of the events from the first draft of your novel. Rather, we are using our first draft as a point of departure, while taking into account the variety of scenes we feel may no longer be required in the next draft, or the scenes that still need to be written, events reordered, information relayed in a more dramatic or clearer way, character inconsistencies clarified, redundancies banished, and so on. All of these factors are taken into account as we write a new outline with a clearer sense of the story. We take our time, pondering our story, granting our imagination the authority to consider the most effective way to tell the story.

DILEMMA

Everything that happens in our story leads to the ending. The goal is that the whole of our story be greater than the sum of its parts, which is to say that our story is about something more than the plot. The plot is simply a vehicle by which we explore a theme, a universal aspect of the human condition.

Everything that happens in our story, whether we are conscious of it or not, explores the dilemma at the heart of our story. Our job now is to be as clear and specific as we can. A dilemma is different than a problem. Problems are solved. Dilemmas are resolved through our protagonist's transformation. In the rewrite we will become increasingly aware of our characters as archetypes and we may begin to see how they all constellate around the dilemma.

TRANSFORMATION

In the rewrite we become conscious of what we have done subconsciously. We are not interested in the three-act structure as a formulaic approach to story that reduces human behavior to simplistic cliché, but rather, as a way to deepen our understanding of our story so that we can recognize the underlying meaning of what our subconscious did so naturally. It is important to remain connected to why we are telling our story, otherwise the rewrite process can actually degrade all of the great work we did in the first draft.

PITFALLS OF THE REWRITE

Within our first draft is a diamond in the rough. The challenge is to know what to expel and what to keep. How often have we given our work to a friend for notes only to receive opinions: 'I like this scene, but not that one.' It's unusual to find someone who reads our work with a genuine curiosity as to what we're attempting to express.

People tend to read with the assumption that this is the final product. The consequence of receiving notes based on one's opinion rather than on a fundamental curiosity about what the writer is attempting to express can lead the writer to lose connection to his work. When we show our work too soon, we are abdicating authority over it. We are basically saying, 'Tell me what to do.' Certainly there comes a point where we need a fresh eye, but until we have done all we can do, we jeopardize our relationship to our initial impulse.

There are all sorts of ways to go off track in our attempt to 'improve' our first draft, and they can be boiled down to one word: Fear.

1. Fear that it will be misunderstood—and so, we 'simplify' the conflict, killing the aliveness of our character's motivations.

2. Fear that it will never be good—we become impatient and rush, because we aren't really sure anything will come of it. It is inevitable that at some point in the rewrite we will grow tired of our work. This is an occupational hazard. Familiarity breeds contempt, and we are going to become very familiar with our words.

3. Fear we are doing it wrong—we become convinced that our process is not valid. We become confused about what to keep, what to remove, where to go from here.

4. Fear that we are wasting our time—this is similar to the fear that it won't be good, but it includes the larger fear that nothing we do will ever be good. This fear can spread like the plague and can run the gamut of creative expressions, until our fear has us where it wants us . . . paralyzed, and awash in self-doubt.

5. Our fears are endless, and are designed to prevent us from completing our work.

PREPARATION

As we approach Day 1 there are a few things I want to suggest in preparation.

1. Read your first draft. It is inevitable that you will want to make changes. Fine. Keep them to a minimum. Just read it and get to the end. Get a sense of what you have written.

2. If you wrote the first draft longhand, start transcribing it. Again, don't worry too much about editing. If there are passages you aren't sure you want to keep, it might be quicker to just transcribe them now and concern yourself with it later. Also, I encourage you to transcribe it yourself and not hire it out. This is your opportunity to re-experience the story.

3. Do not talk about your story to people, friends and loved ones included. Wait until you have a first draft.

4. Commit to a daily routine. We are creatures of habit. If possible, try to write at the same time each day.

5. Commit to writing two hours a day.

6. This is a major undertaking. If we make our 90-Day Rewrite a top priority for the next three months we will be in a better frame of mind to handle whatever life throws our way.

I look forward to guiding you through this process.

Your fellow writer,
AL WATT
LA Writers' Lab
imagine. create. transform.